SpringerBriefs in Computer Science

SpringerBriefs present concise summaries of cutting-edge research and practical applications across a wide spectrum of fields. Featuring compact volumes of 50 to 125 pages, the series covers a range of content from professional to academic.

Typical topics might include:

- A timely report of state-of-the art analytical techniques
- A bridge between new research results, as published in journal articles, and a contextual literature review
- A snapshot of a hot or emerging topic
- An in-depth case study or clinical example
- A presentation of core concepts that students must understand in order to make independent contributions

Briefs allow authors to present their ideas and readers to absorb them with minimal time investment. Briefs will be published as part of Springer's eBook collection, with millions of users worldwide. In addition, Briefs will be available for individual print and electronic purchase. Briefs are characterized by fast, global electronic dissemination, standard publishing contracts, easy-to-use manuscript preparation and formatting guidelines, and expedited production schedules. We aim for publication 8–12 weeks after acceptance. Both solicited and unsolicited manuscripts are considered for publication in this series.

**Indexing: This series is indexed in Scopus, Ei-Compendex, and zbMATH **

Zili Meng · Mingwei Xu

Latency Optimization in Interactive Multimedia Streaming

 Springer

Zili Meng
Department of Electronic and Computer
Engineering
Hong Kong University of Science
and Technology
Hong Kong, Hong Kong

Mingwei Xu
Department of Computer Science
and Technology
Tsinghua University
Beijing, China

ISSN 2191-5768 ISSN 2191-5776 (electronic)
SpringerBriefs in Computer Science
ISBN 978-981-97-6728-1 ISBN 978-981-97-6729-8 (eBook)
https://doi.org/10.1007/978-981-97-6729-8

This Springer imprint is published by the registered company Springer Nature Singapore Pte Ltd.
The registered company address is: 152 Beach Road, #21-01/04 Gateway East, Singapore 189721,
Singapore

If disposing of this product, please recycle the paper.

Preface

In the rapidly evolving digital age, interactive multimedia streaming has become an indispensable part of our everyday lives. From video conferencing and live broadcasts to online gaming and virtual reality, the demand for seamless and instantaneous multimedia experiences continues to grow. However, meeting the stringent latency requirements of these applications remains a formidable challenge within the Internet's architecture.

This book is born out of the doctoral dissertation work, which has been awarded the Doctoral Dissertation Award from ACM China, Chinese Institute of Electronics, and Tsinghua University—it worths a read. Over the course of our research, we have identified and systematically addressed the various facets of latency fluctuations, proposing innovative solutions to optimize performance across different layers of the Internet architecture. The journey has been intellectually challenging and immensely rewarding, and I am excited to share these insights with a broader audience.

The core contributions of this work are multifaceted. We propose a novel architecture for interactive multimedia transport that tackles the heterogeneous latency contributors by separately optimizing the control path and data path. This architectural framework is critical for understanding and mitigating the root causes of latency fluctuations. This book aims to provide a comprehensive guide on optimizing latency for interactive multimedia streaming. It is intended for researchers, engineers, and practitioners in the field of multimedia communications, as well as anyone interested in understanding the intricacies of Internet architecture and performance optimization. By sharing the methodologies and practical implementations, we hope to contribute to the ongoing efforts to enhance interactive multimedia streaming technologies.

We invite you to embark on this exploration of latency optimization in interactive multimedia streaming. May the insights and solutions presented here inspire further innovations and advancements in this dynamic and vital field.

Hong Kong   Zili Meng
Beijing, China   Mingwei Xu
May 2024

Contents

Acronyms

ABR	Adaptive Bitrate
ABRF	Available Bandwidth Reduction Factor
ACK	Acknowledgement
AMPDU	Aggregate MAC Protocol Data Unit
AP	Access Point
AQM	Active Queue Management
AR	Augmented Reality
CCA	Congestion Control Algorithm
CCDF	Complementary Cumulative Distribution Function
DMR	Deadline Miss Ratio
ECN	Explicit Congestion Notification
EWMA	Exponential Weighted Moving Average
EWMV	Exponential Weighted Moving Variance
FCT	Flow Completion Time
FEC	Forward Error Correction
FIFO	First-In-First-Out
FQ	Fair Queue
JFI	Jain's Fairness Index
LTE	Long-Term Evolution
MAC	Media Access Control
MCS	Modulation and Coding Scheme
MDP	Markov Decision Process
MTU	Maximum Transmission Unit
NSDI	Conference on Networked System and Design and Implementation
PLT	Page Loading Time
PSNR	Peak Signal-to-Noise Ratio
QoE	Quality of Experience
RED	Random Early Detection
RTC	Real-Time Communication
RTT	Round-Trip Time
SIGCOMM	ACM Special Interest Group in Data Communication

SSIM	Structural Similarity
TCP	Transmission Control Protocol
UDP	User Datagram Protocol
VR	Virtual Reality
WAN	Wide Area Network
WLAN	Wireless Local Area Networks

Chapter 1
Introduction

Abstract This chapter gives an introduction to interactive multimedia streaming, and highlights the problems and recent works.

Keywords Interactive multimedia streaming · Ultra-low latency video streaming · Real-time communications · Network latency

1 Interactive Multimedia Streaming

The Internet has become an indispensable part of our lives. Whether it is for work, study, socializing, or entertainment, our daily activities depend on the Internet. In particular, over the past two to three decades, with the continuous upgrading of network technology, cellular networks have gradually been deployed from 2G to 5G, and wireless local area networks (WLAN) have gradually been deployed from WiFi-4 to WiFi-7, greatly enhancing the speed and bandwidth of the Internet. This has led to an increasingly diverse range of Internet applications, extending from traditional text and image transmission to multimedia streaming. Nowadays, it is difficult for people, from urban to rural areas, to imagine life without the Internet. According to statistics, 59.7% of the world's population were long-term Internet users in 2022, with an average monthly data usage of 49.8GB and an average Internet speed of 75.4 Mbps [1]. Among them, multimedia streaming applications, including audio, video, images, text, and other multimedia data, are an essential Internet component. By 2022, multimedia traffic had reached 82% of the total Internet traffic [1].

Interactive multimedia streaming applications are applications that stream multimedia content (e.g., video, audio) to users while interacting with users at the same time. For example, videoconferencing is a typical example of interactive multimedia streaming applications. Users receive the video and audio contents from the Internet, and users' reactions will be encoded into video and audio and sent back as well. Especially since the outbreak of the COVID-19 pandemic, the interactive nature of multimedia streaming has attracted increasing attention. These interactive multimedia streaming applications have been extensively applied in various scenarios, such as teaching and remote collaborations.

Z. Meng and M. Xu, *Latency Optimization in Interactive Multimedia Streaming*,
SpringerBriefs in Computer Science, https://doi.org/10.1007/978-981-97-6729-8_1

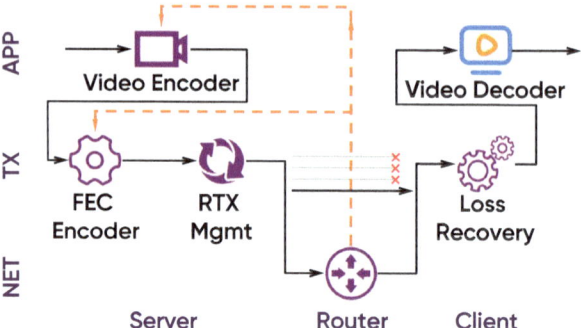

Fig. 1 Overall structure of interactive multimedia streaming

Subsequently, emerging interactive multimedia streaming applications have also garnered widespread attention. The interactive multimedia streaming has expanded into cloud gaming, virtual reality, remote healthcare, and many other areas, extending from traditional person-to-person calls to human–machine interaction control and beyond. Some common scenarios include holographic video conferencing, cloud gaming, virtual reality, remote healthcare, and industrial control. For example, with cloud gaming, the gaming application will run on the cloud instance instead of the client PC, and gaming content will be streamed from the cloud to users in video format. In virtual reality (VR) and augmented reality (AR), the contents rendered on the headset must follow users' interactions as well to ensure a seamless experience.

In summary, Fig. 1 illustrates the overall structure of interactive multimedia streaming. As multimedia streaming is inherently a network application, we divide it vertically into application, transport, and network layers from the perspective of the Internet architecture and horizontally into servers, routers, and clients. The contents rendered on the server will first be encoded with video encoders (e.g., H.264). The encoded data will later be handed to the transport layer stack, going through the loss recovery modules, such as the encoder for forward error correction (FEC) and the manager for retransmission. Later, the data will go to the Internet through a series of routers and reach the client. The client has all the counterparts to the server in all layers, where the data will reversely go up from the network layer to the application layer and finally be displayed to the user.

The interactive multimedia streaming has received widespread attention in academia in recent years. International conferences in the fields of networking (e.g., SIGCOMM and NSDI) and multimedia (e.g., MM and MMSys) have published numerous papers on optimization in this direction. In the industrial sector, many open-source and closed-source frameworks have emerged. The most famous example is the WebRTC from Google, with many variants customized by different companies such as Alibaba's AliRTC, Agora's AgoraRTC, and Tencent's TRTC. The research works in this book are also compatible with WebRTC for reproducibility convenience.

2 The Fragile User Experience: Latency Fluctuation

Latency is the most crucial metric for interactive multimedia streaming as it directly correlates with user experience. Interactive multimedia streaming applications not only require low latency but also demand stability in latency. For example, let's imagine a scenario where wireless users usually experience satisfactory round-trip delays of less than 100 ms. However, if the 99th percentile of network round-trip delays exceeds 400 ms, the network latency will far surpass the application's latency budget [2, 3]. In this case, one out of every 100 packets may experience high latency, severely affecting the user experience. Therefore, reducing tail latency and stabilizing latency fluctuations are paramount for interactive multimedia streaming applications.

2.1 Strict Deadline Requirements

As interactive multimedia streaming applications continuously interact with humans, controlling end-to-end latency is essential for achieving a satisfactory user experience. For instance, video conferencing aims for an end-to-end latency of less than 130 ms [4, 5], while cloud gaming strives for a latency of less than 96 ms [6]. The numbers are based on the statistics of most users, while different users and applications may have varying sensitivity to latency. For example, for gaming applications, 3D games have stricter latency requirements than 2D games [7]. In practice, server-side and client-side processing typically requires approximately 30 ms [8–11]. Therefore, the end-to-end round-trip delay of the network should not exceed 50–150 ms (depending on the application), which constitutes the application's deadline [12, 13].

We conducted a measurement on a typical cloud gaming service. During the measurement, the round-trip interaction latency of each video frame was categorized into several intervals. This allowed us to study users' tolerance for different latencies. When users experience higher interaction latency and terminate their sessions due to an inability to tolerate such high latency, the frames with high interaction latency will be very close to the end of the user's session. Therefore, this measurement analyzes users' reactions to latency by examining the distribution of frames with different latency. Figure 2 shows the distribution of frame positions in the stream for each category, where the x-axis represents the position of the frame in a session, normalized by the total duration of the session. For example, a position of 99% indicates that the frame appears very close to the end of the session. If a line is constant between 0% and 100% (e.g., the solid lines in the figure), these frames appear uniformly throughout the session. Conversely, the three dashed lines in the figure indicate that these frames are more likely to appear at the end of the session. Compared to the uniform distribution of low-latency frames (solid lines), frames with latency greater than 100ms (dashed lines) have a higher probability of appearing at the end of the stream. We conjecture that this is because users tend to terminate sessions when experiencing higher latency. This also suggests that as long as packets

Fig. 2 Distribution of frame
locations for different
latencies

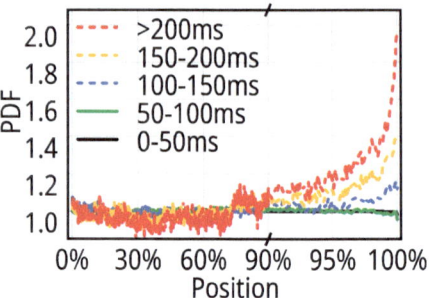

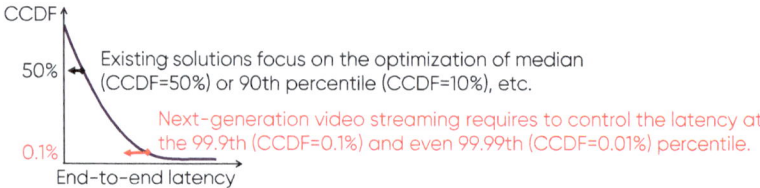

Fig. 3 This book focuses more on the optimization of extreme tail latency control for interactive
multimedia streaming

can be transmitted within the deadline (approximately 100 ms in this case), faster
delivery will not significantly impact the user experience.

Therefore, the deadline miss rate (DMR) should be minimized to achieve a
seamless user experience in interactive multimedia streaming. For example, the
example above shows an interaction latency deadline of approximately 100 ms.
For interactive multimedia streaming, this deadline miss rate must be reduced to an
extremely low level. Even if the DMR is 10^{-3}, it would decrease user experience for
one out of every 1000 frames. This is still bad—when the frame rate is 60 fps, the
interval of having a decrease in user experience is merely 16.7 s. Such an occurrence
of every tens of seconds would still significantly degrade the user experience [13].

The focus on the extreme tail percentiles of latency in this book differs from
the focus of existing work. Figure 3 provides a perspective on latency distribution
(complementary cumulative distribution function, CCDF), with traditional work generally focusing on the more common 50th percentile latency (and sometimes the 90th
percentile). However, 10^{-3} implies that we need to focus on the 99.9% percentile
latency, which presents a new set of requirements and optimization spaces.

2.2   Unsatisfactory Status-Quo Performance

However, the current network performance, especially wireless access network performance, is unsatisfactory at the tail when the goal is the latency at the 99.9%
percentile or even further. Several recent observations support this view. First, exist-

Table 1 Recent relevant measurement results on wireless network latency

Narayanan et al. [14]	Tail latency of 5G hops has not improved much compared to 4G, and can be as high as 200 ms
Daldou et al. [15]	The average WiFi hop latency of 802.11ax (also known as WiFi 6) is greater than 30ms with 30 interferers
Bhartia et al. [16]	Up to a quarter of 802.11a wireless access points suffer from >100 ms latency on the last hop
Ghoshal et al. [17]	For median users, 5G millimeter wave does not improve maximum latency much compared to 4G LTE

ing literature reveals that even when using advanced access technologies, wireless networks exhibit long tail latencies. We summarize recent measurement results in Table 1. Even with WiFi 6 (802.11ax) or 5G (millimeter wave), wireless networks still perform poorly. This is consistent with the feedback from some content providers. Also, it is not uncommon to read reminders such as "We recommend that customers use wired networks to access cloud desktops." from cloud service providers. Google Stadia's user guide states, "If you encounter network problems, please plug your computer into a wired Ethernet connection if possible" [18]. Latency-sensitive applications find that users prefer inconvenient but stable wired networks due to the high tail latency of wireless networks.

Additionally, our measurements reveal a decline in wireless network tail performance. We measured an online real-time communication service (AliRTC) that serves millions of users daily and showed the network conditions and application performance of wired, WiFi, and 4G access networks. Frame delay refers to the latency measured at the application layer, where we will use this concept multiple times throughout this book. As shown in Fig. 4, wireless networks can usually provide satisfactory round-trip latencies (far less than 100 ms). However, the 99th percentile round-trip latency for wireless networks exceeds 400 ms, far surpassing the application's latency budget [2, 3]. In this case, one out of every 100 packets may experience high latency, severely affecting the user experience. Application layer metrics show a similar pattern: wireless users encounter video latency twice (long frame delays) as Ethernet users. Moreover, the frame rate drop (video stutter) ratio for wireless networks is ten times that of wired networks.

While a wireless network behaves much worse than a wired network, it is impractical to rely on the wired network fully all the time. For virtual reality, no one will prefer to have a headset connected via a cable to the workstation. For autonomous driving, connecting the car to somewhere with a cable will be even infeasible. Using a separate frequency band in wireless communication is not very practical, considering the time-consuming battles to fight for a new frequency band. The whole interactive multimedia streaming delivery pipeline must learn to work with such fluctuations all the time.

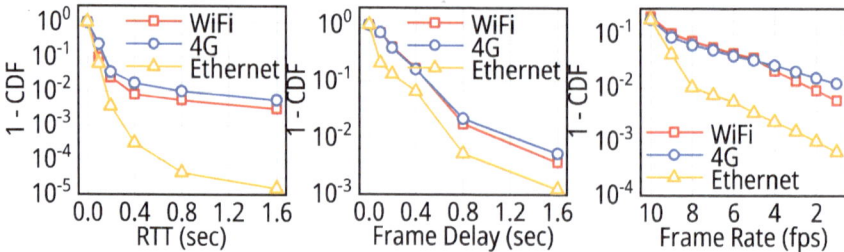

Fig. 4   Round-trip latency, frame delay, and frame rate distribution on WiFi, 4G, and wired networks

3   Book Content

While the root cause sounds to be the fluctuation of the wireless network, the issue will also be propagated to all the other components on the pipeline. For example, when the network capacity is unavoidably degraded due to wireless interferences, the video encoder must accordingly reduce the encoding bitrate to match the new capacity and avoid overshooting the network. Loss recovery, congestion control, and all the other components in the delivery pipeline must also react to any fluctuations in the network. Therefore, this book is not a wireless communication book but introduces how the whole delivery pipeline of interactive multimedia streaming will react to network fluctuations.

This book begins by examining Internet architecture and conducting a comprehensive analysis of the sources of latency fluctuations in the new generation of multimedia transmission. The study encompasses the complete process of identifying, defining, and resolving the issue. Initially, the research focuses on the latency fluctuations in the new generation of multimedia transmission, conducting a thorough analysis and identifying the impact of multiple links in the Internet architecture on latency fluctuations. Subsequently, the study optimizes the causes of latency fluctuations in these links, delving into an in-depth investigation from the application layer to the network layer of the protocol stack. The following sections briefly introduce the main content of each part of the study.

3.1   *Interactive Multimedia Streaming Architecture*

Before analyzing the latency issues in interactive multimedia streaming, it is essential to understand the sources of latency. This book systematically proposes possible sources of latency fluctuations in interactive multimedia streaming, highlighting the impact of *control path* and *data path* latency on overall end-to-end latency. The study first analyzes the life of a video frame from rendering to playback, breaking down each component. Additionally, the possible interactions between different components are examined. The study can optimize each component individually through a comprehensive analysis and modeling of the interactive multimedia streaming architecture.

In this context, the control path refers to the passage of control information, specifically the control loop's response to performance fluctuations in the network. If the endpoint responds too late to network fluctuations, latency fluctuations may result from bandwidth mismatches. The data path refers to the route a data packet itself takes, encompassing the application, transport, and network layers. If latency fluctuations occur at any stage, the overall end-to-end latency of the data packet will fluctuate accordingly. The detailed work is presented in Chap. 2.

Note that this book is not going to introduce all possible solutions at each component like an encyclopedia. Instead, we will only introduce one solution in detail to showcase how the research in that component can be conducted and briefly cover several pieces of related work. We recommend the readers to check the references for more information.

3.2   Control Path Latency

In analyzing and optimizing control path latency, this book focuses on the feedback and decision-making components. These two components' latency fluctuations and reliability directly affect the end-to-end latency of data packets.

Feedback refers to the process by which the signal of "fluctuation occurrence" in the network reaches the sender. When the network's available bandwidth changes at a specific moment, the sender cannot instantly understand this change—the transmission of this message takes time. For example, in the TCP protocol, messages are usually transmitted through ACK packet delay or delivery rate changes. In this case, the feedback time requires at least one round-trip delay. The detailed work is presented in Chap. 3.

Decision-making refers to the process from the sender's initial receipt of the network fluctuation signal to the sender's response. If the sender only observes one or two signals of network fluctuations, it may not take them seriously-network noise is substantial, and changes in one or two packets may be mistaken for noise. For example, many congestion control algorithms only make decisions after observing a specific network change for a continuous RTT or even longer. However, if the decision-making process is too conservative, the decision might be late to the network as well. In this case, the timeliness and reliability of decisions are crucial. The detailed work is presented in Chap. 4.

3.3   Data Path Latency

In the analysis and optimization of data path latency, this book primarily focuses on the application, transport, and network layers, which are the upper layers in the network architecture. The latency fluctuations in each of these layers directly affect the end-to-end latency of data packets.

Application layer latency generally includes data processing and queuing delays at the application layer. For example, at the receiving end, once the data has been sequenced by the transport layer, if the application cannot promptly process and retrieve the data, the data must be queued at the application layer, waiting for processing. In this situation, this queuing will result in increased end-to-end latency. This issue becomes increasingly severe as the processing speed of the application becomes slower—the resolution and frame rate are increasing simultaneously. Consequently, active management of application layer latency is necessary. The detailed work is presented in Chap. 5.

Transport layer latency is primarily caused by packet loss recovery. A data packet may be lost during transmission due to queue overflow or wireless network interference, resulting in the packet being damaged and unable to pass verification to reach the receiver. In this case, the sender must promptly identify the packet loss event and retransmit the lost data packet. However, both the identification of packet loss and the process of retransmitting lost data packets generate additional latency. Additionally, due to the "best-effort" nature of internet design, packet loss is often challenging to avoid. As interactive multimedia streaming latency requirements become increasingly stringent, reducing transport layer latency is also necessary. The detailed work is presented in Chap. 6.

Network layer latency is generally caused by mismatches in queue rates and bandwidth. In network queues, multiple users' traffic shares (or competes for) the same resource-bandwidth. The traffic characteristics of other users are often difficult for the current user to predict in advance. For example, if other users competing with an interactive multimedia streaming stream suddenly increase their transmission rate, the available bandwidth for the interactive multimedia streaming traffic will typically decrease. Of course, congestion control algorithms will converge to a new steady state. However, as attention to tail latency increases, even the fluctuations in this convergence process can lead to a decline in end-to-end latency and corresponding user experience. The detailed work is presented in Chap. 7.

References

1. Cisco vni complete forecast highlights global—consumer highlights. https://www.cisco.com/c/dam/m/en_us/solutions/service-provider/vni-forecast-highlights/pdf/Global_Device_Growth_Traffic_Profiles.pdf (2022)
2. Jason Livingood. Working latency-the next qoe frontier-apnic blog. https://blog.apnic.net/2021/12/02/working-latency-the-next-qoe-frontier/ (2021)
3. Mohan, N., Corneo, L., Zavodovski, A., Bayhan, S., Wong, W., Kangasharju, J.: Pruning edge research with latency shears. In Proc, ACM HotNets (2020)
4. Jones, A., Sevcik, P., Wetzel, R.: Internet connection requirements for effective video conferencing to support work from home and elearning | netforecast. https://www.netforecast.com/wp-content/uploads/NFR5137-Videoconferencing_Internet_Requirements.pdf (2021)

5. Meng, Z., Guo, Y., Sun, C., Wang, B., Sherry, J., Liu, H. H., Xu, M.: Achieving consistent low latency for wireless real time communications with the shortest control loop. In: Proc. ACM SIGCOMM (2022)
6. Kämäräinen, T., Siekkinen, M., Ylä-Jääski, A., Zhang, W., Hui, P.: A measurement study on achieving imperceptible latency in mobile cloud gaming. In Proc, ACM MMSys (2017)
7. Ivkovic, Z., Stavness, I., Gutwin, C., Sutcliffe, S.: Quantifying and mitigating the negative effects of local latencies on aiming in 3d shooter games. In: Proc. ACM CHI, pp. 135–144 (2015)
8. ArsTechnica. Nvidia gtx 1080 review: the new performance king. https://arstechnica.com/gadgets/2016/05/nvidia-gtx-1080-review/4/ (2016)
9. Shi, S., Hsu, C.-H., Nahrstedt, K., Campbell, R.: Using graphics rendering contexts to enhance the real-time video coding for mobile cloud gaming. In Proc, ACM Multimedia (2011)
10. GFXBench. 3d graphics performance of google pixel c. https://gfxbench.com/device.jsp?D=Google+Pixel+C (2017)
11. Wimmer, R., Schmid, A., Bockes, F.: On the latency of usb-connected input devices. In: Proc. ACM CHI, pp. 1–12 (2019)
12. Slivar, I., Skorin-Kapov, L., Suznjevic, M.: Cloud gaming qoe models for deriving video encoding adaptation strategies. In Proc, ACM MMSys (2016)
13. Optimizing 5g for a new class of low-latency experiences [video]. https://www.qualcomm.com/news/onq/2021/07/20/optimizing-5g-new-class-low-latency-experiences (2021)
14. Narayanan, A., Ramadan, E., Carpenter, J., Qingxu Liu, Yu., Liu, F.Q., Zhang, Z.-L.: A first look at commercial 5g performance on smartphones. In Proc, WWW (2020)
15. Daldoul, Y., Meddour, D.E., Ksentini, A.: Performance evaluation of ofdma and mu-mimo in 802.11 ax networks. Comput. Netw. (2020)
16. Bhartia, A., Chen, B., Wang, F., Pallas, D., Musaloiu-E, R., Lai, T.T.T., Ma, H.: Measurement-based, practical techniques to improve 802.11 ac performance. In: Proc. ACM IMC (2017)
17. Ghoshal, M., Dash, P., Kong, Z., Xu, Q., Hu, Y.C., Koutsonikolas, D., Li, Y.: Can 5g mmwave enable multi-user ar apps? In: Proc. PAM (2022)
18. Troubleshooting your stadia experience - stadia help. https://support.google.com/stadia/answer/9595943 (2021)

Chapter 2
Interactive Multimedia Streaming Architecture

Abstract When the optimization goal of interactive multimedia streaming applications shifts to tail latency, the main contributors of latency are no longer the same as the contributors of median latency in the original architecture. In this chapter, we focus on analyzing where the end-to-end latency fluctuations come from in the existing interactive multimedia streaming architecture. We will analyze the reasons for latency fluctuations in general and then analyze the causes of latency fluctuations from the perspectives of the control path and data path.

Keywords Interactive multimedia streaming · Control path · Data path · Real-time communications

When the optimization goal of interactive multimedia streaming applications shifts to tail latency, the main contributors of latency are no longer the same as the contributors of median latency in the original architecture. In this chapter, we focus on analyzing where the end-to-end latency fluctuations come from in the existing interactive multimedia streaming architecture. We will first analyze the reasons for latency fluctuations in general and then analyze the causes of latency fluctuations from the perspectives of the control path and data path.

1 Reasons of Latency Fluctuation

With the deployment of edge nodes and improvements in network congestion control mechanisms, network latency is no longer the main contributor to end-to-end latency. The current reality is that in many interactive multimedia streaming applications, application service providers can achieve average or median latency as low as 10–15 ms through heavy investment.

Tips
Ping youtube.com from your laptop and see how long the RTT is in your region.

For example, service providers in applications like cloud gaming deploy servers intensively onto multiple nodes, even in one province or region. In this case, for most users, there is likely a computing node in their city to provide services. This is also known as multi-access edge computing (MEC) [1] or content delivery network [2], which greatly shortens network latency. Similarly, as access network technology upgrades from 4G to 5G and WiFi 4 to WiFi 6, the wireless link transmission latency of the last-hop access network has also been greatly improved.

However, when the focus of interactive multimedia streaming shifts to the tail latency of one in a thousand or one in ten thousand, any small fluctuation in any link may cause the end-to-end latency to rise. The existing interactive multimedia streaming architecture has considered adapting to fluctuations in different network situations during design, but not enough attention has been paid to the transition and convergence process from one state to another. This is natural—when the latency percentile of concern is at the 50th or even 90th percentile, there is no need to worry about these transient convergence processes since they only account for a tiny portion of all the time, and most times, the network is stable. However, when the application focuses on these tail latency percentiles, these transient convergence processes become crucial. Therefore, this section mainly analyzes the possible contributors of latency fluctuations when interactive multimedia streaming focuses on the tail latency and the deadline miss rate of one in a thousand.

One important source of latency fluctuations found in this work is the presence of control path latency. As mentioned earlier, network conditions constantly fluctuate, so the endpoint response needs to be constantly adjusted based on network conditions. However, due to the presence of the *control loop*, the response at the endpoint is often delayed. Formally, the response action $a(t)$ at the endpoint at time t is not based on the network state $s(t)$ at time t, but on the network state $s(t - \tau_{\text{control}})$ at time $t - \tau_{\text{control}}$, where τ_{control} is the control path latency. Therefore, when the network state changes, the response action $a(t)$ at the endpoint often lags behind the network state change, leading to end-to-end latency fluctuations.

This becomes very important when the focus of applications shifts from latency to tail latency. In the past, as long as the endpoint could make the correct response, parameters such as the sending rate could converge to the new steady-state value. But network fluctuations do occur occasionally. In some real wireless network data, the probability of network bandwidth dropping to 1/50 of the original may be as high as 1% (Chapter 3). In this case, the control path latency becomes crucial.

At the same time, the roles of different components in the data path in end-to-end latency also change. With the deployment of edge data centers and the emergence of new access network technologies such as 5G and WiFi 6, network end-to-end latency at the median (in general) can even be achieved at 10–20 ms [3]. In this case, when we observe that the latency of a video frame rises to hundreds of milliseconds, the possible cause is no longer just the long physical distance between the two parties. Latency fluctuations at the application, transport, and network layers can lead to instantaneous latency increases.

The remaining two sections of this chapter will analyze these two aspects. Figure 1 shows some components in the interactive multimedia streaming architecture that

$$t_{control} \approx t_{feedback} + t_{decision}$$
$$(\S3) \qquad (\S4)$$

$$t_{data} \approx t_{APP} + (1+RTX) \cdot t_{RTT}$$
$$(\S5) \qquad (\S6) \quad (\S7)$$

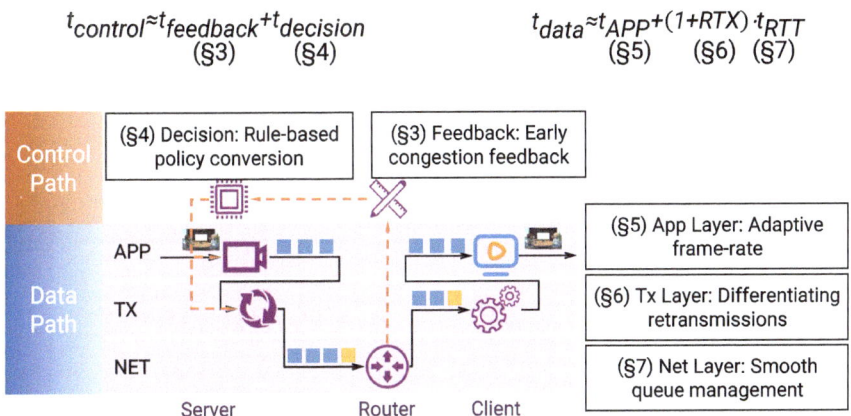

Fig. 1 Interactive multimedia streaming architecture and the roadmap of this book

may affect latency jitter after modeling and analysis. In the control path, feedback latency and decision latency will affect the latency of the control path itself. In the data path, latency at the application layer, transport layer, and network layer will also affect the end-to-end data latency in the data path. The several works involved in this book are also carried out in these two aspects, aiming to systematically solve the problem of latency fluctuations in interactive multimedia streaming.

2 Control Path Delay

This section first identifies the significant role of the *control path* in causing fluctuations in tail-end-to-end delay. The impact of the control path on the delay of interactive multimedia streaming is indirect and only comes into play when the application focuses on tail delay: if the sender adjusts its sending rate *slower* when the network condition changes, the overshooted packets into the network may cause delay fluctuations. Do not underestimate this little response time: if the sender needs hundreds of milliseconds to respond each time the network condition changes, the user experience in these hundreds of seconds will be poor. However, the Internet is always fluctuating—if the network status fluctuates slightly every few minutes, it means that users have a few thousandths of opportunities to encounter performance degradation caused by delay fluctuations. In this case, the delay of the control path becomes crucial.

Figure 2 shows an illustrative example. On the Internet, the available bandwidth of a flow may fluctuate at any time due to wireless channel interference and changes in competing traffic patterns. At this time, the sender's sending rate needs to change accordingly to adapt its throughput to the current available bandwidth in real time. Without loss of generality, when the available bandwidth of an interactive multimedia

Fig. 2 An example of control path delay when available bandwidth drops

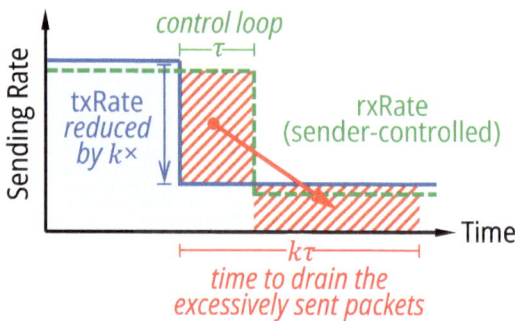

streaming flow at the bottleneck router (solid line) suddenly drops to $1/k$ of the original, the sender's sending rate also needs to be reduced as soon as possible to adapt to the new available bandwidth. However, as mentioned earlier, the sender cannot immediately know the reduction in available bandwidth. It takes a control path delay τ (i.e., control loop) to reflect the decline in the sending rate ultimately. In this case, the reduction of the sender's sending rate will be offset to the right by the reduction of the available bandwidth, as shown by the dashed line in the figure. The solid line in Fig. 2 is the available bandwidth of the bottleneck router, the dashed line is the sending rate of the bottleneck router, and the red shadow is the backlog of the bottleneck queue. During this time, the bottleneck queue still receives packets at the original sending rate, but its processing rate is greatly reduced due to the drop in available bandwidth. Therefore, these excessive packets will cause a backlog in the bottleneck queue, as shown by the red shadow.

What's worse is that when the control path delay is τ, the time users experience the deterioration of delay is likely to be much more than τ. This is another important observation about the control path delay—when the network condition fluctuates due to the fact that the available bandwidth of the network is actually deteriorating, these packets exceeding the network's carrying capacity need several times the original accumulation time to be cleared. Here, we further analyze this example in Fig. 2. Specifically, the packets arriving at the bottleneck queue need k times the time $(k\tau)$ to be sent out during the control loop τ. This is because the data rate sent before the drop in available bandwidth is much higher than the new available bandwidth after the drop. Therefore, the data that may have accumulated in 1 time unit originally takes k time units to alleviate. This is like what is shown in the figure, where the area of the two red shadows in the figure is actually equal. During this time, all sent packets will experience increased delays, thereby reducing user experience.

Specifically, the delay of the control path is divided into two parts: feedback delay and decision delay:

$$t_{\text{control}} = t_{\text{feedback}} + t_{\text{decision}} \tag{1}$$

where the feedback delay t_{feedback} refers to the transmission time of the feedback signal from the sender to the receiver, and the decision delay t_{decision} refers to the time for the sender to make a decision based on the feedback signal. The jitter of these two links may cause fluctuations in the final end-to-end delay. This section first introduces the functions of these two parts and then discusses how they affect the final end-to-end delay fluctuations.

End-to-end performance fluctuations caused by feedback delay jitter How to obtain feedback information is an important problem that almost all control systems face. From error correction adaptation to the sending rate adaptation in interactive multimedia streaming, feedback in decision-making is always critical. This is also reflected in the analysis of many existing works in the network field. For example, QCN [4] assumes that the QCN signal sent by the switch in the network needs to be obtained by the sender after τ time when analyzing stability. Therefore, this feedback delay is actually ubiquitous.

End-to-end control algorithms rely on timely access to network status. For example, TCP congestion control algorithms determine the degree of network congestion based on packet delay, packet loss, and rate changes over a period of time. When network status changes, this change will be immediately reflected in indicators such as packet delay, throughput, and packet loss rate. However, when the network status fluctuates, these indicators often cannot be immediately known by the sender. In this instant process, the mismatch between the sending rate of the sender and the network status will cause end-to-end performance fluctuations. In this context, existing work has the following two shortcomings

First, existing work generally assumes that the feedback delay is constant. This can greatly simplify many modeling and analyses. However, an important observation in Chap. 3 of this book is that in the tail case, the feedback delay actually expands with the expansion of the data path delay. This is because, above the network layer, control information does not have a separate control path but also needs to be transmitted through the data path. Therefore, if the data path causes delay expansion due to packet queuing and other reasons, the feedback delay will also expand with it. This will cause the sender to know the network status change later, further worsening the end-to-end delay.

Second, existing work mainly focuses on stability rather than performance in analyzing feedback delay. The existence of the feedback loop is essential for many stability analyses: generally speaking, if the feedback loop is too long, so much so that it is longer than the cycle of network status changes, then the control system is likely to be non-convergent. However, in the current Internet, the feedback loop is generally much smaller than the network status change. For example, the general feedback loop is about a round-trip delay, which is about tens of milliseconds in general interactive multimedia streaming applications. Network status generally does not change dramatically every few tens of milliseconds, so the usual analysis results are stable [4]. However, when interactive multimedia streaming focuses on the 99.9th percentile or even later delay requirements, the delay fluctuations in the convergence process will also affect user performance.

Chapter 3 provides a detailed analysis of this and proposes a mechanism to stabilize feedback delay by decoupling the data path and control path. As shown in Fig. 1, Chap. 3 will introduce an example of how to optimize the feedback delay $t_{feedback}$ of the control path. The main approach is to decouple control information from the original data packets, unlike traditional protocols that carry control information in the original data packets. In this way, no matter how the data path delay fluctuates and expands, the control path delay can still remain relatively stable. In this case, the sender can always know the current network status relatively timely and make corresponding adjustments.

Rate adjustment lag or error due to unstable decision-making After obtaining network status information, decision-making is another important issue faced by interactive multimedia streaming control algorithms. Signals in the network are often full of noise and ambiguity. For example, when the sender observes a packet loss event, it could imply that the sender needs to reduce the sending rate to alleviate network congestion; or it may simply represent a decrease in the channel quality of the wireless link, but the sender does not need to reduce the sending rate [5]. Therefore, decision-making algorithms tend to make decisions only when sufficient information is collected to have enough confidence.

In recent years, due to the continuous pursuit of performance by applications, the decision logic of congestion control, video bitrate adjustment, and other control algorithms has become more and more complex. Starting from traditional heuristic methods that can be implemented in just a few lines of code, researchers have gradually turned to using neural networks [6, 7] or integer programming [8] for decision-making. These attempts are beneficial: on the one hand, researchers have a deeper understanding of network conditions, and they can optimize the modeling and formulation for the network. On the other hand, inspired by the progress of neural networks and other emerging machine learning technologies in computer vision and natural language processing, researchers tend to believe that these neural networks have great potential in interactive multimedia streaming. However, these newly proposed, sophisticated decision-making algorithms face some problems in the following two dimensions

First, the decision delay of the decision-making algorithm is increasing. The most direct drawback of using neural networks or integer programming algorithms is their extremely high decision-making delay. Traditional heuristic algorithms can be implemented in just a few lines of code and hardly consume much decision time when running in online deployments. However, even in the inference stage, neural networks consume a lot of computing resources. For example, traditional congestion control generally updates the congestion window every time a packet is received. In a flow with a throughput of 30 Mbps (this is a typical bitrate for interactive multimedia streaming), the average interval between two packets is 0.4 milliseconds. However, the forward prediction of neural networks may still consume milliseconds of delay even if specialized acceleration hardware such as GPUs is used. This will only be more severe in mathematical formulation methods such as integer programming optimization. Complicated integer programming may take several minutes or even hours to solve. This shows a gap between the current high decision-making delay and the need for high-frequency decision-making in interactive multimedia streaming control algorithms.

Second, the complexity of the decision-making logic of these algorithms is difficult for network administrators to understand. For example, neural networks usually contain thousands (sometimes even billions [9]) of neurons and output their decision results through complex calculations. Administrators generally have difficulty understanding how a decision is made. In those popular applications like ChatGPT, this might be fine—no one will die because of ChatGPT's responses. However, in interactive multimedia streaming, where decisions must be extremely reliable, this does not work. When decisions may be wrong and not discovered, how can network administrators trust such a model? This is similar for optimization algorithms such as integer programming. When the solution result deviates significantly from the administrator's common sense, the administrator has no way of knowing which constraint or variable design is problematic. In this case, the wrong decision will also cause end-to-end performance fluctuations.

Chapter 4 analyzes the above two problems and proposes an algorithm that can avoid end-to-end performance fluctuations due to unstable decision-making by converting complex algorithms into lightweight, stable decision trees. As shown in Fig. 1, Chap. 4 will mainly cover the topics of optimizing the decision-making delay t_{decision} of the control path. The main approach is to decouple offline optimization from online deployment and no longer bind offline optimization with online deployment as in existing work. Network administrators can still use the algorithms and models they think have high performance and good results for optimization when training offline. However, when deploying this optimized model online, the method can convert it into a decision tree model with low decision delay and interpretability with negligible performance degradation. In this case, the delay and reliability of the decision part can be guaranteed in most cases.

3 Data Path Delay

For the delay on the data path, we first qualitatively analyze the components of the end-to-end delay. Ideally, the delay in the data path is affected by the following factors:

$$t_{\text{data}} = t_{\text{app}} + (1 + \text{RTX}) \times t_{\text{RTT}} \tag{2}$$

Here, t_{app}, RTX, and t_{RTT} represent the application layer processing time, the number of retransmissions, and the round-trip time, respectively. They correspond to the impact of the application, transport, and network layers on the end-to-end delay in the data path. Specifically, we first introduce how the (possible) design flaws in these three layers affect the end-to-end delay in the data path.

- t_{app} is the application layer processing time, which is mainly related to the design of the application layer—for example, if the application layer needs to encode video frames, the encoding time will increase.
- RTX is the number of retransmissions, which is mainly related to the design of the transport layer's packet loss recovery—for example, if a packet is lost RTX times, it will arrive at the receiver on the $RTX + 1$-th transmission.
- t_{RTT} is the round-trip time, which is mainly related to the design of the network layer's queue management - for example, the longer the queue in the network, the longer the round-trip time.

For example, suppose a data packet is first processed by the encoder at the sender for 5 ms (application layer). Then, the data packet starts to be prepared for transmission in the transport layer. The current network RTT is 30 ms. Unfortunately, this data packet is always dropped in the network until the 3rd retransmission, when it successfully arrives at the receiver and is acknowledged. Assuming that the sender can always detect the packet loss within 1 RTT. Therefore, in the transport layer, the total time consumed by this data packet is $(1 + 3) \times 30$ ms=120 ms. After arriving at the receiver, there may be some additional delay in the application layer. For example, the decoding of the video may take 10 ms. Thus, according to the formula 2, the total end-to-end delay is approximately 15 ms + $(1 + 3) \times 30$ ms=135 ms.

Equation 2 is based on a series of approximations. For example, with the existing loss detection mechanisms, the sender may not be able to detect the loss of a data packet immediately. In fact, TCP needs to wait for the successful arrival and acknowledgment of the next three data packets after the first packet loss to trigger the fast recovery mechanism. After the second loss, it will only retransmit the packet again after the retransmission timeout (RTO), which is usually 200 ms (Linux) or 1 s (IETF recommendation). So, the above formula is just a lower bound estimation of the end-to-end delay—the main purpose here is to give you a sense of how different components will affect the end-to-end delay.

Note that the fluctuation of these three components will also lead to fluctuations in the final end-to-end delay. In recent years, some changes have occurred in these components for interactive multimedia streaming applications.

1. Application layer delay: Increased video quality leads to fluctuations in the encoding and decoding processes One significant change in interactive multimedia streaming is the waiting time at the interface between the application and the protocol stack (e.g., socket buffer) can be longer. The existing application layer design does not consider that the bottlenecks might be in the application instead of the network— the current socket buffer in the operating system passively waits for the application to read data from it without actively managing the queue. When the application can handle the data sent by the network in time, the application will actively read data from the buffer. When the application is temporarily unable to handle this data, the data will accumulate in the buffer and wait to be processed. As the available buffer space gradually decreases, the current TCP protocol will adjust the advertised window accordingly to inform the sender to reduce the amount of data to send. When the buffer is full, the receiver will no longer receive new data from the network until the application processes some data to free up space.

However, this design faces a straightforward problem: if the application cannot process the data in time, the queue will continue to accumulate until it is full. This is similar to the situation in the network where the router's queue, if not actively managed, will accumulate until it overflows, resulting in high queuing delays. Such a drop-tail queue design is not friendly to low-latency applications, including interactive multimedia streaming.

The problem of this queue becomes more severe with the development of interactive multimedia streaming applications. As the new generation of multimedia demands higher image quality, the computational complexity of video encoding and decoding also increases. For example, the resolution has evolved from 240p in the past to 1080p today, and in the future, interactive multimedia streaming might have even higher resolutions, such as 4K and 8K. The frame rate of the video has also increased from about 24 fps for video calls to 60 fps, 90 fps, or even higher. This will increase the burden of application processing, leading to fluctuations in end-to-end delay.

Based on this, Chap. 5 covers a detailed analysis of the above problem and later introduces an application layer queue management mechanism as an example. It can actively control the queue in front of the application when a bottleneck occurs, thereby avoiding fluctuations in end-to-end delay. Especially in the increasingly popular high-definition and high-frame-rate interactive multimedia streaming, adopting such a mechanism becomes increasingly urgent. As shown in Fig. 1, Chap. 5 mainly covers the work of optimizing the application layer delay t_{app} in the data path. The main method is to actively manage this buffer queue instead of waiting for it to overflow passively. Like the active queue management algorithm on the router, when the socket buffer starts to grow, the application layer protocol notifies the sender to reduce the sending rate to avoid the buffer accumulating. This way, the application layer delay can be effectively controlled, reducing the fluctuation of the end-to-end delay.

2. Transport layer delay: The increased demand for delay fluctuation makes the existing packet loss recovery mechanism suboptimal As for the transport layer delay, we notice that when the focus on the delay percentile increases from the 50th percentile to the 99.9th percentile, and 99.99th percentile, existing packet loss recovery mechanisms at the transport layer can no longer meet this requirement. Some transport layer designs do not consider the delays that are caused by small probability events such as packet loss. In that context, when data packets are not lost, there are no problems with delay. However, if a data packet is unfortunately lost, the current design of the transport layer is to trigger the fast recovery mechanism after the first time, but it may have to wait for one second to trigger the timeout retransmission after the second time. Although many designs try to speed up this process (e.g., TLP [10]), retransmission is still inevitable. When more extreme situations occur, the delay of data packets in these extreme situations may be very poor. For example, if the packet loss rate in the network reaches 10%, a data packet needs to be transmitted 4 times to reach the receiver. In this case, the delay of this data packet will increase by 4 times.

And at a packet loss rate of 10%, the probability of a data packet being transmitted 4 times (i.e., being dropped 3 times in a row) is $10\% \times 10\% \times 10\% \times 90\%=0.09\%$, which is not negligible. This will directly affect the user experience at the 99.9th percentile.

It is worth noting that, especially for video frames in interactive multimedia streaming, a frame can only be delivered to the application for decoding when all data packets of the frame have arrived at the receiver. That is to say, if a video frame has 50 data packets, even if one data packet is dropped, as described above, the user's experience will still be affected by this video frame. Therefore, the existing packet loss recovery mechanism is difficult to meet the extreme requirements of the new generation of multimedia transmission for delay jitter.

This problem has also become more severe with the development of interactive multimedia streaming applications. Game users may be able to tolerate a stutter rate of 1/1,000, but applications like remote surgery and remote-assisted driving require a 1/10,000 or even lower stutter rate. Imagine a complex surgery or a long-distance trip that lasts for hours, and even a few seconds of stuttering can be fatal. These few seconds in ten hours are roughly equivalent to a 1/10,000 or even lower stutter rate requirement. At the same time, as the bitrate increases but the data unit (Maximum Transmission Unit, MTU) in the network does not increase accordingly, the phenomenon of a video frame containing multiple data packets and blocked by one missing packet in the aforementioned problem becomes more severe. Therefore, it is important to reconsider these applications that mainly rely on packet loss recovery and did not properly consider tail delay fluctuations during design.

Based on this, Chap. 6 also provides a detailed analysis of the above problem, supported by measurement data, and introduces a recent piece of work on a transport layer packet loss recovery mechanism. This mechanism can significantly alleviate the end-to-end delay jitter of interactive multimedia streaming caused by packet loss and retransmission and, at the same time, reduce bandwidth costs. As shown in Fig. 1, the works in Chap. 6 will mainly optimize the transport layer delay in the data path, i.e., its retransmission times RTX. The main method is to combine two common packet loss recovery mechanisms (forward error correction and retransmission) to increase the redundancy rate when the time budget is running out (e.g., the 2nd and 3rd transmissions) to avoid extremely adverse situations. In this way, the effective control of end-to-end delay fluctuations caused by small probability events can be achieved.

3. Network layer delay: The diversity of congestion control algorithms leads to performance fluctuations in network layer queue management mechanisms We notice that in recent years, the traffic characteristics and application requirements faced by network layer queue management mechanisms have also changed. As mentioned earlier, the main source of delay in the network layer is queuing. The cause of queuing is generally due to the mismatch between the arrival rate and the sending rate of the queue. In traditional network layer queue management, algorithms like CoDel [11] limit the length of the queue to avoid excessive delay due to long queues and have been widely deployed. However, these algorithms face the following two problems under the traffic characteristics of today's network transmission:

First, the response of queue management algorithms is more focused on packet loss rather than other indicators. Current queue management algorithms, when designed initially, targeted traditional loss-based TCP congestion control algorithms, such as Reno [12] and CUBIC [13]. The most prominent feature of these algorithms is that they rely on packet loss signals (or ECN signals) to adjust the rate. For example, when the sender does not observe packet loss, it will continue to try to increase the sending rate (or congestion window). Only when the sender observes packet loss will it reduce the sending rate. However, interactive multimedia streaming applications no longer use loss-sensitive congestion control algorithms but use delay-sensitive congestion control algorithms like GCC [14] to achieve low latency. This means that existing queue management algorithms are not effective in controlling delay: delay-sensitive congestion control algorithms no longer respond to packet loss signals. Ensuring low latency at the network layer is no longer simple.

Second, the design of queue management algorithms focuses more on long-term performance rather than short-term performance. For example, in terms of fairness, researchers measure throughput fairness metrics (e.g., Jain's fairness index) on a long time scale of tens or hundreds of RTTs. However, how to gradually converge to this fairness in the transient state is mostly neglected. As mentioned earlier, the transient performance of the convergence process is critical when the focus of performance shifts to tail delay. Especially when some competing traffic in the network (e.g., web browsing) is always fluctuating, the network layer queue management mechanism can hardly control the delay as expected. Consequently, users will suffer a poor experience at the tail.

Based on this, Chap. 7 analyzes the transient performance of queue management algorithms and the response signals of congestion control algorithms. As shown in Fig. 1, Chap. 7 will mainly optimize the network layer delay t_{net} in the data path. We find that as web design becomes more complex and application performance requirements become more diverse, the mechanisms in Chap. 7 will play an increasingly important role. Later, we introduce an active queue management mechanism within the network layer that controls performance fluctuations by limiting the instantaneous interference of burst traffic on stable traffic. On the one hand, the main approach is to no longer rely on packet loss signals but on delay in conveying information to congestion control algorithms. Conversely, smoothly transiting during different states allows congestion control algorithms to have sufficient time to respond. In this way, the queue management mechanism can effectively control delay fluctuations when network traffic and other fluctuations occur.

References

1. Taleb, T., Samdanis, K., Mada, B., Flinck, H., Dutta, S., Sabella, D.: On multi-access edge computing: a survey of the emerging 5g network edge cloud architecture and orchestration. IEEE Commun. Surv. Tutorials (2017)

2. Corneo, L., Eder, M., Mohan, N., Zavodovski, A., BayhanZ, S.: Surrounded by the clouds. In Proc, WWW (2021)
3. China Mobile and ZTE. Powered by sa: 5g mec-based cloud game innovation practice. GSMA 5G Case Studies (https://www.gsma.com/futurenetworks/wp-content/uploads/2020/03/Powered-by-SA-5G-MEC-Based-Cloud-Game-Innovation-Practice-.pdf) (2020)
4. Alizadeh, M., Kabbani, A., Atikoglu, B., Prabhakar, B.: Stability analysis of qcn: the averaging principle. In Proc, ACM SIGMETRICS (2011)
5. Dong, M., Li, Q., Zarchy, D., Brighten Godfrey, P., Schapira, M.: Re-architecting congestion control for consistent high performance. In Proc. USENIX NSDI, Pcc (2015)
6. Abbasloo, S., Yen, C.Y., Chao, H.J.: Classic meets modern: a pragmatic learning-based congestion control for the internet. In: Proc. ACM SIGCOMM (2020)
7. Mao, H., Netravali, R., Alizadeh, M.: Neural adaptive video streaming with pensieve. In Proc, ACM SIGCOMM (2017)
8. Yin, X., Jindal, A., Sekar, V., Sinopoli, B.: A control-theoretic approach for dynamic adaptive video streaming over http. In Proc, ACM SIGCOMM (2015)
9. Brown, T., Mann, B., Ryder, N., Subbiah, M., Kaplan, Jared D., Dhariwal, P., Neelakantan, A., Shyam, P., Sastry, G., Askell, A., Agarwal, S., Herbert-Voss, A., Krueger, G., Henighan, T., Child, R., Ramesh, A., Ziegler, D., Wu, J., Winter, C., Hesse, C., Chen, M., Sigler, E., Litwin, M., Gray, S., Chess, B., Clark, J., Berner, C., McCandlish, S., Radford, A., Sutskever, I., Amodei, D.: Language models are few-shot learners. In H. Larochelle, M. Ranzato, R. Hadsell, M.F. Balcan, and H. Lin, editors, Advances in Neural Information Processing Systems, volume 33, pages 1877–1901. Curran Associates, Inc. (2020)
10. Cheng, Y., Cardwell, N., Dukkipati, N., Jha, P.: The RACK-TLP Loss Detection Algorithm for TCP. IETF RFC 8985 (2021)
11. Nichols, K., Jacobson, V.: Controlling queue delay. Communications of the ACM (2012)
12. Padhye, J., Firoiu, V., Towsley, D.F., Kurose, J.F.: Modeling tcp reno performance: a simple model and its empirical validation. IEEE/ACM Trans. Netw. **8**(2), 133–145 (2000)
13. Ha, S., Rhee, I., Xu, L.: Cubic: a new tcp-friendly high-speed tcp variant. ACM SIGOPS Operating Syst. Rev. (2008)
14. Carlucci, G., De Cicco, L., Holmer, S., Mascolo, S.: Congestion control for web real-time communication. IEEE/ACM Trans. Netw. (2017)

Chapter 3
Feedback on Control Path: Early Congestion Feedback

Abstract We introduce Zhuge, a novel approach to reducing tail latency in wireless networks by minimizing the control loop for congestion feedback. Wireless networks often suffer from transient congestion due to sudden drops in available bandwidth, causing high end-to-end latency. Existing solutions are limited by the delayed feedback loop inherent in current network designs. Zhuge addresses this by decoupling the control loop from the congested path, allowing quicker reaction to bandwidth fluctuations. It features a Fortune Teller module that predicts packet delays and a Feedback Updater that modifies upstream packets, ensuring consistent low latency without requiring modifications to the sender or receiver.

Keywords Congestion control · Congestion feedback · Wireless router · Interactive multimedia streaming

1 Introduction

Transient congestion at wireless links is caused when available bandwidth for a user drops suddenly, *e.g.,* due to multi-user access and mutual interference. The available bandwidth of wireless networks can drop by $10\times$ at the 99th percentile (§2.3). After such a sudden drop, packets quickly begin to queue at the AP, increasing end-to-end latency. Ideally, senders would react quickly when bandwidth reduction occurs, *e.g.,* by reducing their bitrate to prevent queue buildup, high latency, and loss. Unfortunately, we observe that senders are *fundamentally limited* in how quickly they can react, and it is *precisely when queues build up that senders react most slowly!*

The problem is that congestion signals are carried along the same congested path as data packets. Put simply, to observe that the bottleneck queue is filling, a sender must first receive an acknowledgment from a packet that has actually *waited in that queue*. Hence, congestion indicators like timestamps or losses take longer to reach the sender when the sender *most needs these indicators*. In Fig. 1, we show the route taken both by data packets and the control signals they carry, in-band/explicitly (such as timestamps) or out-of-band/implicitly (such as their RTT).

© The Author(s), under exclusive license to Springer Nature Singapore Pte Ltd. 2024
Z. Meng and M. Xu, *Latency Optimization in Interactive Multimedia Streaming*,
SpringerBriefs in Computer Science, https://doi.org/10.1007/978-981-97-6729-8_3

23

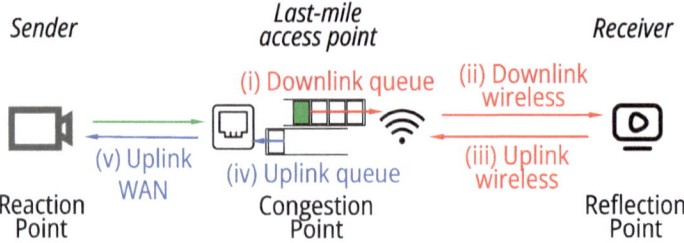

Fig. 1 Control loop for rate adaption at the wireless last mile. Compared with existing solutions, Zhuge bypasses the segment (i) - (iii) to achieve the shortest control loop

Our key insight in this chapter is that we can decouple the control loop from the full path that data packets traverse, hence protecting control signals from experiencing the full latency of filling, often buffer-bloated [1] queues. A carefully designed AP, on observing a filling downlink queue (i in Fig. 1), can modify or delay packets in the uplink queue (iv in Fig. 1), allowing congestion signals to reach the sender without the delay of the congested bottleneck.

Substantial research literature aims to improve network latency for wireless networks, but these approaches primarily succeed at improving *median* rather than *tail* latencies of RTC applications in the wireless network. We argue that the problem primarily stems from all of these approaches relying on a delayed control loop due to congestion signals needing to traverse the congested, high-latency path. For example, end-based solutions such as congestion control algorithms (CCAs) collect end-to-end signals (e.g., per-packet delays) at the sender to adjust the sending rate. However, one (inflated) control loop is still needed to collect the signals after sending a packet. Similarly, in-network solutions such as active queue management (AQM) create signals (e.g., packet drops), but these signals still have to be bounced by the receiver to the sender, which suffers a long control loop.

While our key insight is straightforward, implementing it successfully in practice is challenging:

How can an AP predict packet latency for packets that have not yet been transmitted?
Naïvely, an AP might simply measure the number of bytes queued in the downlink queue and divide by the available link capacity to measure a queuing delay. However, recall that link bandwidth fluctuates (hence our problem), so such an estimator is likely to be inaccurate.

How should the AP report the message back to the sender in a deployable way?
A straightforward solution is enabling routers to directly transmit newly defined messages back to senders (e.g., XCP [2] or active network [3]). However, coordinating AP and senders that are usually maintained by different entities (§2.3) builds barriers for deployment at scale. Moreover, for existing deployed protocols at the sender, some use explicit signaling (e.g., timestamps), while others use implicit or out-of-band signaling (e.g., the RTT or RTT gradient). Some protocols react to a

weighted moving average of the RTT [4]; some protocols are concerned with minimum RTT values over a particular window [5]; and some protocols react to inter-packet timings and are not concerned with RTT at all [6]. The AP must modify or delay upstream packets in a way that faithfully captures all of these factors so that neither the sender nor the receiver requires modification.

Addressing these challenges, this chapter presents Zhuge[1] (pronounced as /'druːgə) that achieves consistent low latency[2] in wireless environments by minimizing the control loop. Zhuge includes a *Fortune Teller* module that, on packet arrival at the downstream queue, makes a *prediction* as to that packet's delay to the receiver and back to the AP. The Fortune Teller separately estimates two factors influencing queuing delay (§4.1) and uses these to derive a combined prediction for every arriving packet. The second component of Zhuge is a *Feedback Updater*, which modifies upstream packets. Depending on the protocol, these modifications are based on either the raw packet delays recorded by the Fortune Teller or *differences of packet delays* (details in §5.2) derived from the Fortune Teller.

2 Background and Motivation

In this section, we use real-world statistics to reveal the status of wireless tail latency (§2.1). Next, we analyze why existing solutions fail to achieve consistent low latency (§2.2). Finally, we present our motivation for reducing the control loop to ameliorate tail latency (§2.3).

2.1 Understanding Wireless Tail Latency

We first answer the following one question: Why does wireless latency fluctuate at the tail?

The outstanding tail latency is caused by the transient mismatch of the sending rate at the sender and available bandwidth (ABW) at the bottleneck queue. As analyzed in §2, the transient increase of latency depends on (i) how violent the ABW fluctuates (k), and (ii) how soon the sender reacts (τ). As for the ABW fluctuation k, wireless channels naturally fluctuate more than wired channels due to their variability.

We calculate the available bandwidth every 200 ms, during which the CCA should respond to such fluctuations considering the RTT. Solid lines represent traces from several open datasets, and dashed lines represent traces from our own mea-

---

[1] Zhuge is a famous fortune-teller in ancient China.

[2] We mainly focus on recent CCAs that are designed to maintain a low latency but fail to achieve a low latency consistently. Buffer-filling CCAs that suffer from a high RTT all the time, e.g., CUBIC [7]) are not our target.

Fig. 2 Distribution of wireless available bandwidth reduction ratio

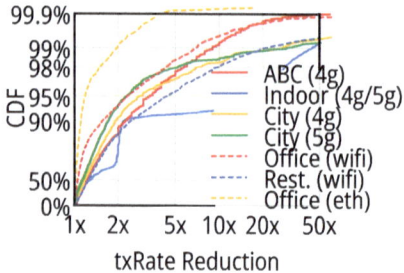

surements in the office and restaurant. The available bandwidth is the average value of each 200 ms measurement window. Considering the typical RTT of the Internet (tens of milliseconds), the congestion control algorithms should react to fluctuations in such a time scale.

As shown in Fig. 2, for all wireless datasets including 5G mmWave and 5GHz-band WiFi, 0.6–7.3% of ABW reduction rates are above $10\times$, which is much higher than the $<0.1\%$ of wired networks. As for the control loop τ, in most cases, the congestion controller needs one RTT to adjust the sending rate upon receiving the congestion signals (e.g., increased delay, packet losses). When the bottleneck queue starts to build up, the end-to-end RTT also inflates, further preventing the congestion signals from reaching the sender. Consequently, the end-to-end latency will fluctuate at the tail.

2.2   Existing Solutions

The reduction of ABW (k) is due to contention in the link layer and below [8] and is unavoidable most of the time (e.g., due to wireless interference). Many transport layer innovations have been proposed to improve the steady-state median latency of a connection. For example, BBR [4] moves the working point of congestion control from a full queue in CUBIC [7] to an empty queue. CoDel [9] queue management also tries to shorten the queue in the steady state in a variety of network conditions compared with FIFO. Subsequent research efforts (including congestion control [5, 6, 10] and active queue management [11]) further provide insightful thoughts on maintaining the optimal working point with different feedback signals. Standing on the shoulders of giants, the median latency for applications can be nicely controlled. However, they are insufficient to reduce the tail latency, which we will analyze below.

End host-based solutions For the network layer and above, existing end host-based solutions fail to quickly adapt to the ABW reduction due to their long and inflated control loops. Recalling Fig. 1, when the green shaded packet arrives at the congestion point and observes a long queue, it first needs to go through the queue (i), transmitted to the receiver (ii), the corresponding feedback delivered from the receiver

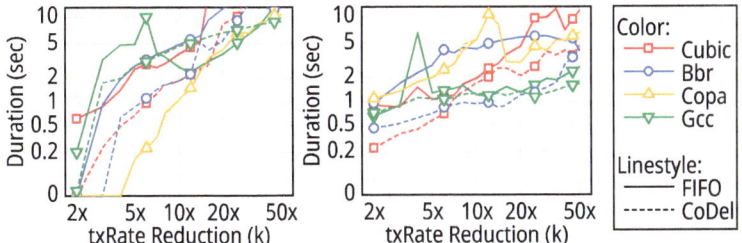

Fig. 3 Convergence duration of (**left figure**) RTT and (**right figure**) CWND after wireless bandwidth drop for different CCAs and AQMs. *RTT degradation duration is the time when RTT > 200 ms. CWND rate reduction duration is the time for CCA re-convergence*

to the access point (iii), and finally sent to the sender (iv and v). Since the shortest time for the sender to be notified is one full control loop, including segments (i)-(v), a pure end host-based CCA cannot adapt to transient bandwidth fluctuation in a timely manner. We further simulate the performance of recent latency-sensitive CCAs (BBR [4], Copa [5], and GCC [6]) together with AQMs in Fig. 3. When the ABW is reduced by 10× or more, all these algorithms, working with or without latency-aware AQMs, suffer from seconds of RTT degradation. The inflated control loop for end host-based solutions results in severe wireless queuing.

In-network solutions Solutions modifying in-network devices also fail to provide timely feedback on these signals. For example, AQM such as CoDel [9] drops the packets in the front of the queue to reduce the downlink queuing latency (i) in Fig. 1, yet still suffers long wireless latency (ii) and (iii), which could be more than 100ms [12]. Moreover, AQMs are mostly designed to *drop* some packets, while many modern CCAs are designed to be responsive to the increase of packet *delay* and insensitive to packet drops [4–6]. This can also be validated in Fig. 3: CoDel can hardly improve the performance of delay-based CCAs such as Copa. There are also solutions to co-design the hosts and in-network routers for decades to achieve better feedback from the network, including XCP [2], RCP [13], Kickass [14], and ABC [15]. However, their design goal is to get a precise estimation of network conditions from routers while the gathered information still needs to go through the full control loop.

2.3 Our Proposal: Reducing the Control Loop

Our key insight to reduce wireless tail latency is to separate the congestion feedback from the congestion by sensing the network conditions as early as possible, timely carrying the conditions back to the sender to *minimize the control loop*, and performing the above operations in a deployable way.

The earliest signal—one packet knows its fortune upon arrival In most cases, when one packet arrives at the bottleneck queue, it can predict its delay with the visibility of the entire queue. For example, the queuing delay for the packet could be roughly estimated by dividing the queue length by the dequeuing rate. Therefore, when the dequeuing rate decreases, we can observe increasing queuing delay upon the arrival of subsequent packets. Compared with other consequent signals, such as the packet loss or the measured queuing delay, the estimated queuing delay is the earliest signal for the reduction of ABW. Therefore, we are motivated to utilize this earliest signal to control the sending rate and adapt to ABW reduction.

Quickly delivering the earliest signal back to the sender Merely finding the ABW reduction signal is not enough. We need to carry this signal back to the sender quickly. An ideal solution is directly *telling* the sender from the bottleneck queue about its current status. In this way, such a signal could bypass the inflated part of the control loop (downlink queuing (i), downlink wireless transmission (ii), and uplink wireless transmission (iii) in Fig. 1). Meanwhile, the latency of the uplink queue at the AP (iv) and the latency of WAN (v) is usually stable. The uplink of the AP is often the Ethernet connection to the Internet, usually with hundreds of Mbps capacity. The WAN latency (v) is the latency between the last-mile AP and the sender. The Ethernet users will also suffer these two parts of the control loop, which are relatively stable according to our Ethernet measurements in Fig. 5.

Patching the last-mile router only might be deployable Reviewing the history of transport layer designs, one can see that there are a series of excellent efforts that, unfortunately, are not widely deployed due to practical issues. For example, XCP [2], RCP [13], Kickass [14], ABC [15], and active network [3] in recent two decades all require modifications on both the server and some or all routers. However, servers are usually controlled by content providers (e.g., Google, Facebook), while routers are by vendors (e.g., Netgear for APs). Coordinating all these parties to push a new transport innovation forward is extremely challenging, if not impossible. Different from the above work, Zhuge patches the last-mile AP only, which could reduce the barrier to deploy at scale. AP vendors could individually implement and observe the performance benefits without cooperation with content providers. Moreover, from the view of home users, the last-mile AP is the only place they can control if they seek a better performance. We are thus motivated to limit the modifications to the last mile to make Zhuge deployable at scale.

3   Zhuge Design

This section presents the design challenges and framework overview of Zhuge to control the wireless tail latency.

3.1 Design Challenges

Zhuge handles wireless tail latency by reducing the control loop. However, Zhuge design confronts two major challenges.

Timely and precise estimation of packet latency for RTC traffic Zhuge estimates the future latency of a packet upon its arrival at the wireless last mile to obtain network conditions as early as possible. A per-packet precise estimation is necessary to properly guide CCAs in the sender for rate adaption. However, precise latency estimation is challenging for RTC traffic in wireless environments, as the bottleneck queue is in a transient fluctuation at a *sub-RTT granularity* for two reasons.

- *Bursty packet arrivals of RTC traffic.* RTC applications generate contents in the unit of a video frame. To reduce the end-to-end latency, senders tend to burstily send packets of the same frame out [16]. This indicates that the queue might build up very quickly, even in a steady state.
- *Bursty packet departures of the wireless channel.* The sharing nature of wireless networks results in the contention of wireless channel resources and frequent bandwidth fluctuation. Wireless protocols tend to aggregate several packets into one MAC frame (e.g., aggregated MAC protocol data unit, or AMPDU, in WiFi) to compromise wireless contention. In this case, tens of packets might be aggregated into one AMPDU and dequeued simultaneously.

A naive estimation approach is simply dividing the queue length by the dequeuing rate. However, this approach is faced with a *transience–equilibrium nexus* [17]: The dequeuing rate is usually measured over a sliding window (e.g., 40ms for WiFi in [15]). A short window would lead to the variability of measurement during the steady state, while a long window misses transient latency fluctuation at sub-RTT granularity. Thus, it is challenging to estimate the per-packet latency for RTC traffic at the wireless last mile in a timely and precise manner.

Effective message feedback for various protocols and CCAs Zhuge notifies the sender of the estimated wireless network conditions as quickly as possible. A straightforward solution is constructing a new type of feedback packet for the sender. However, network conditions such as the current available bandwidth are not explicitly delivered on the Internet for most CCAs deployed in the wild. Directly telling the sender the network conditions would require modifications at the sender simultaneously to make the message understandable to the CCA. As mentioned above, we prefer an AP-based solution without modifying the sender for deployability at scale.

Making this challenging, transport protocols and CCAs adopted by real-world applications are highly diversified. The headers of transport protocols could be unencrypted (e.g., TCP) or encrypted (QUIC). To achieve lower latency, RTC applications prefer to customize CCAs, which rely on different signals to adjust the sending rate. For example, some of them modify the TCP CCA in the kernel [18]. For

WebRTC-based applications, network conditions are periodically summarized into a special feedback packet [19]. Various CCAs make it challenging to effectively deliver the network conditions to the sender.

3.2   Framework Overview

In response to the above challenges, we design two building blocks in Zhuge: a *Fortune Teller* and a *Feedback Updater*.

To achieve timely and precise prediction of packet latency, we introduce the Zhuge Fortune Teller in §4 to tell the fortune (future latency) of each packet upon its arrival. To overcome the transience–equilibrium nexus and faithfully obtain precise per-packet latency, we break the latency into different parts and introduce long-term and short-term estimators. We measure the average dequeuing rate to calculate the long-term queuing delay and the packet sojourn time at the front of the queue to respond to short-term fluctuations.

To effectively notify the sender with the latest conditions, we present the Zhuge Feedback Updater in §5 to convert predicted network conditions to signals that senders can understand. We categorize existing protocols in RTC applications into out-of-band feedback and in-band feedback. For out-of-band feedback protocols, the arrival of feedback packets are signals to the sender (e.g., ACK packets in TCP). In-band feedback protocols carry network conditions in the payload of feedback packets, such as the transport-wide congestion control feedback (TWCC-FB) packets in WebRTC [20]. Accordingly, Zhuge designs different feedback mechanisms to carry the latency back to the sender for a variety of protocols.

The overall workflow of Zhuge is presented in Fig. 4. When a packet arrives at the wireless access point via the Ethernet port, Fortune Teller will predict its fortune and forward the packet as usual to the downlink queue. Feedback Updater will then update the estimation into the feedback packets in the reverse direction. If a newly arrived packet observes a degraded network condition (e.g., increasing queue length), estimated wireless latency could be immediately applied to feedback packets in the reverse direction of the same flow. In this way, the earliest signals could be

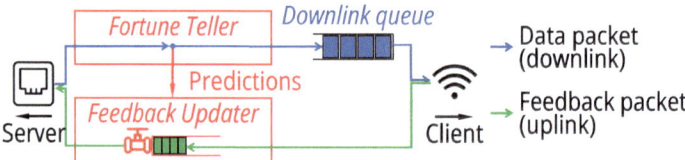

Fig. 4 Overall workflow of Zhuge at the last-mile AP. Zhuge contributes the Fortune Teller and Feedback Updater

carried back to the sender, bypassing the queuing delay and wireless transmission delay of the control loop (part (i)-(iii) in Fig. 1).

4 Fortune Teller

Telling the fortune of a packet is to predict when it will arrive at the client, *i.e.*, the subsequent delay it will experience. In a wireless network, such delay can be decoupled into two segments [21], including (i) Queuing delay: the delay between the packet arriving at the access point and the packet leaving the queue disciplines to the underlying driver (i.e., the delay in the network layer). (ii) Transmission delay: the delay between the packet being passed to the wireless driver to the time it arrives at the receiver (i.e., the delay in the link layer). Next, we introduce how to predict these two delays in a timely manner.

4.1 Queuing Delay Prediction

As discussed in §3.1, the strawman solution of dividing the queue size by the dequeuing rate confronts the transience–equilibrium nexus. A short sliding window will lead to drastic fluctuations of the predicted delays due to the bursts of arrivals and departures, and a long window will fail to detect the change in network conditions quickly. In response, we analyze how to capture the latency fluctuation incurred for the two reasons respectively.

- *Bursty packet arrival of RTC traffic.* The bursty RTC traffic quickly builds up the wireless queue. Our design choice is to predict the packet fortune for each packet instead of on a periodic basis. In this way, the delay differences within a burst of RTC traffic can be captured by taking the queue size observed by each packet as input.
- *Bursty packet departure of the wireless channel.* Bursty packet departure introduces transient glitches to the dequeuing rate at the millisecond timescale, which is easily averaged and, therefore, missed with existing sliding window-based measurements. Our main observation is that when the dequeuing rate is suddenly reduced, an instantly measurable signal is the *waiting time of the packet at the front of a queue* (denoted as the front packet). For example, when the channel starts to become busy, the packet at the front of the queue has to wait for more time to get a chance to be transmitted.

Since the causes of delay are different when the packet is at the front of the queue and is not, we decouple the queuing delay into two parts: long-term queuing delay (qLong) and short-term queuing delay (qShort), as shown in Fig. 5. Specifically, qLong is defined as the delay from when one packet arrives to when that packet is at

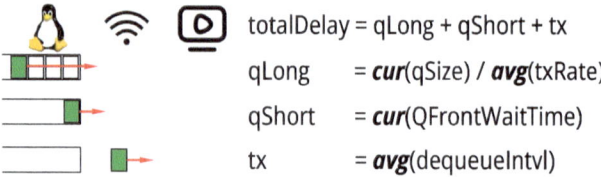

$$\text{totalDelay} = \text{qLong} + \text{qShort} + \text{tx}$$

qLong	$= \boldsymbol{cur}(\text{qSize}) \,/\, \boldsymbol{avg}(\text{txRate})$
qShort	$= \boldsymbol{cur}(\text{QFrontWaitTime})$
tx	$= \boldsymbol{avg}(\text{dequeueIntvl})$

Fig. 5 Different delay components that the Fortune Teller will estimate. qLong and qShort together form the queuing delay at the network layer. tx is the transmission delay at the link layer

the front of the queue, which is used to cover the latency fluctuation induced by wireless contention and bursty RTC traffic. We could estimate qLong as the ratio of current queue size over the average dequeuing rate since it's more affected by the queue dynamics. Short-term queuing delay is the time from when one packet is at the front of the queue to when that packet is finally dequeued. qShort is more related to the sending pattern at the link layer (e.g., the aggregation of MAC data units will lead to fluctuations in qShort). We therefore individually predict qLong and qShort, and take their sum as the estimation of queuing delay. In Fig. 5, $avg(\cdot)$ denotes the *average* value over a sliding window, while $cur(\cdot)$ denotes the *current* value measured at the time of calculation. $qSize$ is the size of the queue, $qFrontWaitTime$ is the time that the current front packet of the queue has waited so far, and $txRate$ is the dequeuing rate of the queue.

Using the combination of long-term and short-term queuing delay prediction has two advantages. We illustrate the advantages with an example in Fig. 6. First, using qShort can quickly detect the ABW drop. When the ABW starts to decrease, since the queue needs some time to build up, and the measured txRate also needs some time to decrease due to the sliding window, qLong increases slowly. Instead, packets have to wait for a longer time to send, which could be immediately observed. As illustrated in 5–15 ms in Fig. 6, qShort would dominate the increase in total queuing delay, quickly reflecting the ABW drop. Second, using qLong could provide a stable and accurate estimate of the queuing delay when the queue has already been built up. For example, when the ABW while the bottleneck queue is still overloaded (e.g., after 15 ms in Fig. 6), qLong would dominate the queuing delay, providing a stable and accurate estimation.

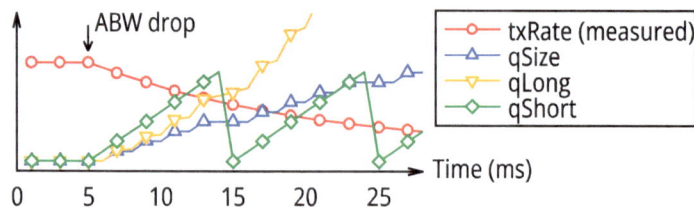

Fig. 6 How qLong and qShort react to the ABW drop at 5 ms

Next, we introduce how we handle two practical issues in the estimation of queuing delay.

Adjustments against bursty departure The bursty departure of the queue due to the aggregation of packets at the link layer could affect the accuracy of the estimation of qLong: when there are several packets in the queue, they may be sent out together at once. In fact, according to our design, fluctuations within a burst should be reflected on qShort. Thus, when calculating qLong, we estimate $qSize$ as

$$qSize = max(\text{sizeOfPacketsInQueue} - \text{maxBurstSize}, 0) \tag{1}$$

where $maxBurstSize$ is the maximum size of simultaneous packet departures at the resolution of 1 ms.

Calculation with queue disciplines Another issue in practice is that queues, in reality, might not be FIFO as assumed in research papers [15]. For example, the default queue discipline in systemd has been changed to fq_codel among different flows differentiated by their 5-tuples [22]. For cellular networks, each flow also has its own queue isolated from competing flows [15]. In these cases, we need to calculate the statistics of the RTC flow's corresponding queue.

4.2   Transmission Delay Prediction

In this section, we mainly target the estimation of delays in the WiFi network. We refer the readers to [15] for the estimation of cellular networks. Predicting the transmission delay for each packet is challenging since it is correlated to the underlying wireless drivers and physical channels. Especially for high-performance wireless devices (e.g., 802.11ax), critical features (e.g., bit-rate selection and frame aggregation) are coded in the hardware device and inaccessible from the access point CPU without significant vendor interaction [12]. For example, many Netgear routers adopt the Qualcomm Atheros hardware [23], where performance-critical features (frame aggregation, etc.) are hard-coded and inaccessible. Therefore, it is challenging to predict the transmission delay of the wireless channel.

According to [15], we summarize the following observations of the transmission delay. First, similar to all link layer protocols, there should be only *one data unit* in transmission in the wireless channel. For example, an 802.11ac sender might aggregate several packets into one data unit (aggregated MPDU, or AMPDU). However, multiple AMPDUs cannot be transmitted simultaneously since their signals will interfere with each other. Therefore, the wireless driver will aggregate several packets into one AMPDU, send it out, and wait for acknowledgment or timeout of that AMPDU. Second, with recent efforts in the Linux mainline, the queue in the lower layers of the wireless network stack has been exposed to the queue discipline [21]. In this case, the lower layer queue in the wireless network stack is only used to aggregate multiple packets into a link layer frame.

Consequently, as shown in Fig. 5, the transmission delay `tx` is calculated as the average interval between packet departures from the network layer queue, with a window similar to txRate. The sliding window should be long enough to cover at least two bursts from the sender so that packets are continuously measured. Note that since multiple packets might be aggregated and dequeued simultaneously, we do not calculate the intervals that are less than one millisecond.

5 Feedback Updater

Zhuge delivers the estimated latency back to the sender in a message that is comprehensible to the sender. To avoid modifications at end hosts, Zhuge abide by the original feedback message format of application protocol and CCAs. This section starts by categorizing feedback mechanisms of popular CCAs for RTC applications (§5.1) and then introduces our corresponding solutions (§5.2 and §5.3).

5.1 Feedback Mechanism Classification

We investigate popular RTC applications and summarize their feedback mechanisms in Table 1. They can be categorized into two types: in-band and out-of-band. We present their behaviors in Fig. 7. Some protocols may utilize both feedback mechanisms. For example, the RTP sender also measures the RTT itself, similar to TCP [19]. This RTT information is not used for rate control but only to stabilize the RTP control loop.

- *In-band feedback*. As shown in Fig. 7, in-band feedback means that the feedback information is explicitly written in the payload of a specific type of feedback packet. For example, the Real-Time Protocol (RTP) and the Real-Time Control

Table 1 We categorize the feedback mechanisms of existing RTC applications into out-of-band feedback and in-band feedback

	Protocol	CCA	Application
Out-of-band (§5.2)	TCP	PCC [10]	Meta Live [25]
	QUIC [24]	BBR [4]	Windows 365 [26]
		Copa [5]	Twitch [27]
			Tencent Start [18]
In-band (§5.3)	RTP+RTCP [19]	GCC [6]	Google Stadia [30]
		NADA [28]	Zoom [31]
		Scream [29]	Microsoft Teams [32]

Protocols of some applications are identified by ourselves

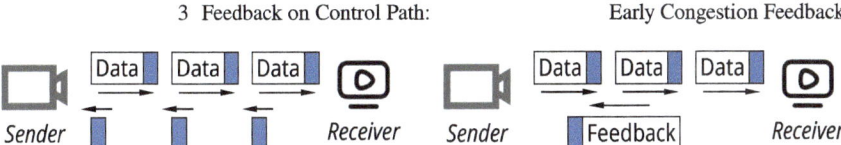

3 Feedback on Control Path: Early Congestion Feedback

Fig. 7 Illustrations of out-of-band feedback (**left figure**) and in-band feedback (**right figure**). Out-of-band feedback protocols do not explicitly carry the feedback information in the payload, while in-band ones do. Blue and white blocks denote packet headers and payloads

Protocol (RTCP) follow the in-band feedback. The receiver records each data packet's arrival time and periodically constructs a feedback packet to carry time intervals back to the sender [20].

• *Out-of-band feedback.* Out-of-band feedback mechanisms do not explicitly write the information related to rate control in the payload of feedback packets. In contrast, the sender calculates all network conditions itself upon receiving the feedback packets. For example, a TCP client will acknowledge each packet it receives. When the sender receives the ACK packet, the RTT, receiving rate, and other network conditions will be calculated.

We separately design solutions for the above two different feedback mechanisms. For out-of-band feedback mechanisms, network conditions are measured only by the sender. Our observation is that we can *deliberately delay* the feedback ACK packets to carry the network conditions back. For in-band feedback mechanisms, as feedback information is written in the payload of feedback packets, we need to update the payload of feedback packets. Next, we introduce two solutions in detail.

5.2   Out-of-Band Feedback: Delaying ACKs

ACK packets are used as messages for applications relying on out-of-band feedback but are consumed in different ways by various CCAs. For example, BBR counts the receiving rate and queries the minimal RTT of ACK packets for rate adaption, while Copa [5] is sensitive to per-packet delay. To satisfy the requirements of different CCAs, our design goal is to faithfully deliver the estimated latency in the finest per-packet granularity by *delaying ACK packets*. CCAs can then aggregate fine-grained information and react in their own ways.

We present an illustration of how Zhuge carries the predicted packet fortunes back from the view of AP in Fig. 8. Blue arrows indicate how network conditions can be sensed by the sender without Zhuge. Assume packets with sequence numbers k and $k + 1$ arrive at the AP from the server, and now the available bandwidth drops. Without Zhuge, the packet behind (seq $k + 1$) will be dequeued later than expected, and the queuing delay will gradually increase ((1) in blue). The client will then receive these two packets with an enlarged interval and consequently acknowl-

edge them with that interval. The ACK packets will then arrive at and depart from
the AP with an enlarged interval ((2) in blue). As shown in Fig. 9, without Zhuge,
the sender can only acknowledge increased RTT when the ACK of delayed packets
arrives at time *deltaDelay*.

With Zhuge, the latency of packets seq k and $k + 1$ could be predicted upon their
arrival ((1') in red). If the Fortune Teller predicts that the delay is increasing, we can
immediately delay earlier ACKs of previous packets that have arrived or will arrive
at the access point. As illustrated by red arrows in Fig. 8, we can deliberately enlarge
the interval between other ACK packets (ACK $j + 1$ and $j + 2$) to timely notify
the sender ((2') in red). In this case, the server can detect the available bandwidth
drops when packets with the adjusted delay arrive at the server ((3') in red). The
RTTs of different packets measured by the server with Zhuge would then be shifted
forward as shown in Fig. 9. Consequently, the control loop of CCAs is reduced by
$(k + 1) - (j + 1)$ (counted in ACK number, the green arrow in Fig. 8). Also note
that Zhuge does not need to look at and match the sequence and ACK number
– the numbers presented here are for illustrative purposes. Instead, Zhuge only
looks at the 5-tuple to identify flows and views the sequence and ACK streams as
blackboxes. In this way, Zhuge could still work even if the transport protocol is
encrypted (e.g., QUIC).

However, downlink data packets and uplink feedback packets arrive at the AP
asynchronously. Thus, it is often impossible to one-on-one map the delay predicted

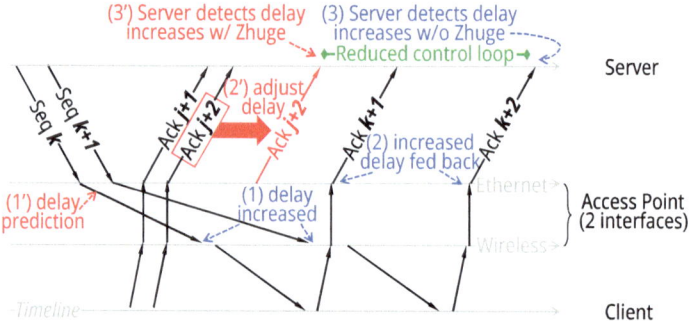

Fig. 8 Zhuge immediately delays the feedback packets in the reverse direction to carry the predicted fortunes back

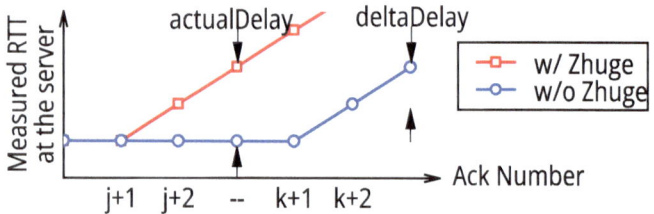

Fig. 9 Zhuge shifts the curve of RTT forward by delaying earlier returning ACK packet to
quickly feedback network conditions. The *actualDelay* is the control loop of Zhuge

by the downlink data packets to the uplink feedback packets. When packets arrive, the Fortune Teller will be updated according to current network conditions. The updated queue conditions include the qLong, qShort, and tx, as introduced in §4. The final predicted total delay is calculated as:

$$totalDelay = qLong + qShort + tx \tag{2}$$

Below, we introduce design principles of Zhuge to ensure the precision of the latency of packets.

Delivering precise long-term latency in the steady state Since Zhuge deliberately delays the feedback packets in the uplink, a natural concern is whether such a delay will affect the estimation of network RTT in the steady state. For example, for the packet seq $k + 1$ in Fig. 8, it has already suffered a long queuing delay in the downlink direction. If Zhuge also introduces a nontrivial delay for its feedback ACK packet ACK $k + 2$ in the uplink direction, it will exaggerate the real RTT and might interfere with the estimation of CCAs.

To handle this problem, we do not directly add the *absolute* estimated delays from the downlink direction into the additional ACK delay in the uplink direction. Instead, we record the *relative delay deltas, i.e.,* the delay difference between consecutive downlink packets. When the estimated delay is increasing, we could record a series of positive delay deltas from the downlink direction and gradually increase the delay in the uplink direction. When the queue has already been steadily built up (e.g., for packets after seq $k + 1$), the delay delta would be around zero, and the feedback packet in the uplink direction would not suffer from additional delays.

Delivering precise short-term latency fluctuation Short-term per-packet latency dynamics are vital for latency-sensitive CCAs like Copa. These CCAs will utilize the patterns of packet delays at the sub-RTT level to control the sending rate. However, naively leveraging the delay delta mechanism may not faithfully deliver short-term latency fluctuations. The reason is that short-term latency varies packet-by-packet. Not every delay delta can be carried in one separate ACK. This might result in the accumulation of multiple delay deltas into one ACK, which is unfaithful. For example, when three data packets arrive at the AP with delay deltas of +1ms between each packet, directly delaying the next ACK for +3ms would introduce a sharper delay increase than the actual value.

To address this problem, instead of delivering per-packet delay delta, our key idea is pursuing the *distributional equivalence* between downlink delay delta and uplink ACK delays. We maintain a distribution of recent delay deltas of the downlink data packets. Upon the arrival of a downlink packet, we calculate the delay delta according to the predicted delay by the Fortune Teller. When an uplink feedback packet arrives at the access point, we *sample* the distribution of recent deltas and use the obtained value to delay the feedback packet. In this case, even under bursty packet arrival and departure, Zhuge is able to mimic the delay distributions to the feedback packets.

Algorithm 1: On data packets: Out-of-band feedback

---

1 deltaDelay = curTotalDelay - lastTotalDelay
2 **if** deltaDelay $\geqslant 0$ **then**
3 | deltaHistory.push_back(deltaDelay)

4 **else**
5 | tokenHistory.push_back(-deltaDelay)

6 lastTotalDelay = curtotalDelay

Algorithm 2: On ACK packets: Out-of-band feedback

---

1 actualDelay = min (0, lastSentTime - curArrvTime)
2 actualDelay += random(deltaHistory)
3 **while** tokenHistory *is not empty* **do**
4 | **if** tokenHistory.front > actualDelay **then**
5 | | tokenHistory.front -= actualDelay
6 | | actualDelay = 0
7 | | **break**

8 | **else**
9 | | actualDelay -= tokenHistory.front
10 | | tokenHistory.pop_front

11 *Schedule to send the current ACK packet after* actualDelay
12 lastSendTime = curArrvTime + actualDelay

Preserving the order of feedback packets Our approach of applying delay deltas to uplink feedback packets introduces an additional challenge of order-preserving of feedback packets. For example, if packet ACK $j + 1$ and $j + 2$ arrive simultaneously, and ACK $j + 2$ samples a lower delay than ACK $j + 1$, the AP may send ACK $j + 2$ in front of ACK $j + 1$, which leads to out-of-order of feedback packets and confusion at the sender. Clamping the sending time of the subsequent packets to the precedent ones, such as holding ACK $j + 2$ until ACK $j + 1$ has been sent, will lead to the overestimation of RTT.

In response, we introduce a delay token to preserve the order of feedback packets and also avoid the overestimation of RTT. When we need to let the subsequent feedback packets wait for the sending of precedent packets, we store the waiting time as a delay token. Next time, when a positive delay delta is sampled, we will first try to consume the token. In this case, the average values of actual delays will be the same as the predicted ones.

We finally present the workflow of how Zhuge Feedback Updater uses the predicted fortune to update the feedback packets. As shown in Algorithm 1, upon arrival of each data packet, given the predicated delay of that packet, Zhuge first calculates the delay delta (line 1). If the delta is nonnegative, we store it in a sliding window. Since Zhuge can only delay the ACK packets with a positive time, if the delta is negative, we need to store it as tokens (lines 4–5). Asynchronously, upon arrival of each ACK packet, Algorithm 2 will be executed to delay ACKs properly. curArrv-

Time is the arrival timestamp of the current ACK, and lastSentTime is the calculated timestamp to send the last ACK packet from the AP to the server. For order preservation, Zhuge first calculates the minimum delay for the current ACK packet to make sure that the current ACK packet would be sent after previous ACK packets (line 1). Zhuge then randomly samples a delay delta from the recent deltas in a sliding window (line 2). Zhuge further checks if there are outstanding tokens and consumes the tokens if available (lines 3–10). Finally, the current ACK packet will be delayed and sent after actualDelay (line 11).

5.3 In-Band Feedback: Updating Payloads

For in-band feedback mechanisms such as RTCP [19], the feedback information (e.g. per-packet receiving time) is written in the payload of feedback packets. We need to update their payloads to carry the freshly estimated latency back to the sender. We use the RTP (data)/RTCP (feedback) protocol pair to introduce how we update the feedback packets with two steps.

- *Step 1: Packet fortune recording.* Upon the arrival of each RTP packet, Zhuge will predict its fortune and then store the predicted delay together with its RTP transport-wide congestion control (TWCC) sequence number in the RTP header.
- *Step 2: Feedback construction.* When it's time to send feedback on the current network conditions back to the sender (e.g., once per RTT or per frame [20]), Zhuge will behave like the RTP receiver and construct a TWCC feedback packet based on stored delays and sequence numbers. To ensure timestamp consistency, Zhuge will only send the TWCC packets constructed by itself and drop all TWCC from the client. For other types of feedback packets (e.g., negative acknowledgment for loss recovery, receiver reports, etc.), Zhuge will forward it from the client to the server as normal.

Detailed RTP/RTCP packet formats are presented in RFCs [19, 20]. Meanwhile, there are two practical concerns regarding the implementation of Zhuge in-band feedback mechanism.

Time synchronization Since the timestamps on the AP may not be synchronized with the receiver, a straightforward concern is whether the time differences between the AP and the receiver would affect the estimation of CCAs. In fact, the server is designed to tolerate the time differences between the server and the constructor of feedback packets (no matter whether clients or APs) since the server is not synchronized with the client either. Therefore, the timestamps of produced TWCC packets are from the same AP clock and consistent with the server.

6 Discussion

Here, we discuss some practical considerations in the deployment of Zhuge and the limitations.

End-to-end encryption In some cases, data packets might be end-to-end encrypted (e.g., SRTP [33] or QUIC). For out-of-band feedback such as QUIC, Zhuge can still work in such cases for the following reasons. First, Zhuge does not need to decrypt the data packet payload. Instead, Zhuge only needs to record the arrival time of each packet. Second, Zhuge does not need to decrypt the feedback packet payload either – it only delays the packet as long as the 5-tuple is still accessible. However, for in-band feedback, Zhuge can no longer work. Zhuge needs to *encrypt* the constructed feedback packet so that the server can correctly decode the packet. In some cases in practice, the server and client share the public key in plaintext with each other at the beginning of the connection [33]. Zhuge might intercept and save the server's public key, and use it to encrypt the constructed feedback. This is a fundamental limitation of Zhuge over RTP/RTCP.

Last-mile *v.s.* **first-mile** We mainly introduce and evaluate the performance of Zhuge in the direction of downlink, where the wireless network serves as the *last-mile*. This is because for many RTC applications such as remote desktop, cloud gaming, and video-on-demand, videos are disseminated from servers to clients. Remote servers, as senders, adjust the sending rate and suffer from a long control loop. For other peer-to-peer RTC applications like video conferencing, the wireless network as the *first-mile* might also introduce tail latency. In this case, queues are built up in the clients. Mechanisms in Zhuge can also be used to handle first-mile tail latency by manipulating the client-side network stack, which needs integration with the application and is beyond our scope.

Fairness Reducing the control loop for a CCA indicates a faster reaction to network conditions, which might imply a greater aggressiveness in both sending rate increase and decrease. A natural concern is whether Zhuge impairs the fairness between optimized flows and other ones. Our answer is *no* because Zhuge does not prioritize target flows by sacrificing others. (1) When *sending rate increases*, wireless queue should be near empty. In this case, flows optimized by Zhuge have a similar control loop to those without Zhuge and will not become more aggressive. (2) *Sending rate decrease* may be caused by wireless queues building up. Zhuge merely reduces the control loop and accelerates convergence, while the converged fairness between different CCAs should be handled during the design of CCAs [34].

Scalability to new protocols In this chapter, we propose solutions for a wide range of applications as long as they use the TCP, QUIC, or RTP/RTCP protocols. However, new protocols may evolve in the future. For new out-of-band protocols, as long as we could identify the flow information from packets, Zhuge could still work from the network layer. For example, since we do not need to know the specific sequence numbers of the packets, even if QUIC encrypts all packets end to end, Zhuge is still able to work with QUIC. For in-band protocols, we need operators to release the format of the protocols to accordingly modify the Feedback Updater in Zhuge.

7 Summary

We introduce the significance of the delay in feedback in network performance and then introduce Zhuge, an in-AP solution that reduces the control loop to alleviate tail latency for interactive multimedia streaming applications in wireless networks. Zhuge predicts the fortune of each packet upon its arrival with the Fortune Teller and quickly notifies the sender about these fortunes over a variety of protocols with the Feedback Updater.

Try it out!
The simulation codes of Zhuge based on NS-3 are available at https://github. com/transys-project/zhuge.

References

1. Winstein, K., Sivaraman, A., Balakrishnan, H.: Stochastic forecasts achieve high throughput and low delay over cellular networks. In Proc, USENIX NSDI (2013)
2. Katabi, D., Handley, M., Rohrs, C.: Congestion control for high bandwidth-delay product networks. In Proc, ACM SIGCOMM (2002)
3. Faber, T.: Acc: using active networking to enhance feedback congestion control mechanisms. IEEE Netw. (1998)
4. Cardwell, N., Cheng, Y., Gunn, C.S., Yeganeh, S.H., Jacobson, V.: Congestion-based congestion control. ACM Queue, Bbr (2016)
5. Arun, V., Balakrishnan, H.: Copa: Practical delay-based congestion control for the internet. In Proc, USENIX NSDI (2018)
6. Carlucci, G., De Cicco, L., Holmer, S., Mascolo, S.: Congestion control for web real-time communication. IEEE/ACM Trans. Netw. (2017)
7. Ha, S., Rhee, I., Xu, L.: Cubic: a new tcp-friendly high-speed tcp variant. ACM SIGOPS Operating Syst. Rev. (2008)
8. Kamerman, A., Monteban, L.: Wavelan®-ii: a high-performance wireless lan for the unlicensed band. Bell Labs technical journal (1997)
9. Nichols, K., Jacobson, V.: Controlling queue delay. Communications of the ACM (2012)
10. Dong, M., Meng, T., Zarchy, D., Arslan, E., Gilad, Y., Godfrey, B., Schapira, M.: Pcc vivace: Online-learning congestion control. In Proc, USENIX NSDI (2018)
11. Høiland-Jørgensen, T., Täht, D., Morton, J.: Piece of cake: a comprehensive queue management solution for home gateways. In Proc, IEEE LANMAN (2018)
12. Bhartia, A., Chen, B., Wang, F., Pallas, D., Musaloiu-E, R., Lai, T.T.T., Ma, H.: Measurement-based, practical techniques to improve 802.11 ac performance. In: Proc. ACM IMC (2017)
13. Tai, C. H., Zhu, J., Dukkipati, N.: Making large scale deployment of rcp practical for real networks. In: Proc. IEEE INFOCOM (2008)

14. Flores, M., Wenzel, A., Kuzmanovic, A.: Enabling router-assisted congestion control on the internet. In Proc, IEEE ICNP (2016)
15. Goyal, P., Agarwal, A., Netravali, R., Alizadeh, M., Balakrishnan, H.: Abc: a simple explicit congestion controller for wireless networks. In Proc, USENIX NSDI (2020)
16. Cinar, Y., Pocta, P., Chambers, D., Melvin, H.: Improved jitter buffer management for webrtc. ACM Trans. Multimedia Comput Commun. Appl. (TOMM) (2021)
17. Liu, S., Ghalayini, A., Alizadeh, M., Prabhakar, B., Rosenblum, M., Sivaraman, A.: Breaking the transience-equilibrium nexus: a new approach to datacenter packet transport. In Proc, USENIX NSDI (2021)
18. Start - tencent cloud gaming. https://start.qq.com/ (2020)
19. Sarker, Z., Perkins, C., Singh, V., Ramalho, M.: Rtp control protocol (rtcp) feedback for congestion control. IETF RFC 8888 (2021)
20. Holmer, S., Flodman, M., Sprang, E.: Rtp extensions for transport-wide congestion control. https://datatracker.ietf.org/doc/html/draft-holmer-rmcat-transport-wide-cc-extensions-01 (2015)
21. Høiland-Jørgensen, T., Kazior, M., Täht, D., Hurtig, P., Brunstrom, A.: Ending the anomaly: achieving low latency and airtime fairness in wifi. In Proc, USENIX ATC (2017)
22. [systemd-devel] [announce] systemd 217. https://lists.freedesktop.org/archives/systemd-devel/2014-October/024662.html (2014)
23. [openwrt wiki] netgear wndr3800. https://openwrt.org/toh/netgear/wndr3800 (2011)
24. Iyengar, J., Swett, I.: Quic loss detection and congestion control. IETF RFC 9002 (2021)
25. Garg, N.: Evaluating copa congestion control for improved video performance. https://engineering.fb.com/2019/11/17/video-engineering/copa/ (2019)
26. Kjerland, E., Shadbolt, M., Watherston, A., Jenks, A., Eby, D.: Network requirements for windows 365 | microsoft docs. https://docs.microsoft.com/en-us/windows-365/enterprise/requirements-network (2021)
27. Shen, Y.: Live video transmuxing/transcoding: Ffmpeg vs twitchtranscoder, part i | twitch blog. https://blog.twitch.tv/en/2017/10/10/live-video-transmuxing-transcoding-f-fmpeg-vs-twitch-transcoder-part-i-489c1c125f28/ (2017)
28. Zhu, X., Pan, R., Ramalho, M., Mena, S.: Network-assisted dynamic adaptation (NADA): a unified congestion control scheme for real-time media. IETF RFC 8698 (2020)
29. Johansson, I., Sarker, Z.: Self-clocked rate adaptation for multimedia. IETF RFC 8298 (2017)
30. Di Domenico, A., Perna, G., Trevisan, M., Vassio, L., Giordano, D.: A network analysis on cloud gaming: Stadia, geforce now and psnow. Network (2021)
31. Marczak, B., Scott-Railton, J.: Move fast and roll your own crypto: a quick look at the confidentiality of zoom meetings - the citizen lab. https://citizenlab.ca/2020/04/move-fast-roll-your-own-crypto-a-quick-look-at-the-confidentiality-of-zoom-meetings/ (2020)
32. Rowe, C., Hanson, D., Craig, C., Coulter, D., Gilmore, J., Byrd, D., Borys, A., Baker, K., Hermansen, B., Soysal, S., et al.: Microsoft teams call flows - microsoft teams | microsoft docs. https://docs.microsoft.com/en-us/microsoftteams/microsoft-teams-online-call-flows (2021)
33. Baugher, M., McGrew, D., Naslund, M., Carrara, E., Norrman, K.: The secure real-time transport protocol (srtp). IETF RFC 3711 (2004)
34. Marfia, G., Palazzi, C. E., Pau, G., Gerla, M., Roccetti, M.: Derivation, analysis, and comparison with other rtt-fair tcps. Comput. Netw. Tcp libra (2010)

Chapter 4
Decision on Control Path: Rule-Based Policy Conversion

Abstract In this chapter, we introduce Metis, a framework designed to convert complex interactive multimedia streaming systems into human-readable control policies. Leveraging decision tree conversion methods, Metis addresses the drawbacks of current decision-making systems, such as their heavyweight nature, incomprehensible structure, and non-adjustable policies. By interpreting deep learning-based adaptive video streaming systems, Metis enables network operators to debug, deploy, and adjust these systems easily. Our approach not only provides interpretability but also reduces runtime overhead, maintaining performance degradation within 2% of the original deep neural networks. We demonstrate Metis's effectiveness through various use cases in system design, debugging, and deployment.

Keywords Interactive multimedia streaming · Decision tree · Rate adaptation · Lightweight decision

1 Introduction

Recent years have witnessed a steady trend of applying deep learning (DL) to a diverse set of network optimization problems, including video streaming [1, 2], local traffic control [3, 4], and network resource management [5–7]. The key enabler for this trend is the use of Deep Neural Networks (DNNs), thanks to their strong ability to fit complex functions for prediction [8, 9]. Moreover, DNNs are easy to marry with standard optimization techniques such as reinforcement learning (RL) [10] to allow data-driven and automatic performance improvement. Consequently, prior work has demonstrated significant improvement with DNNs over hand-crafted heuristics in multiple network applications [1, 3, 11].

However, the superior performance of DNNs comes at the cost of using millions or even billions of parameters [8, 12]. This cost is fundamentally rooted in the design of DNNs, as they typically require numerous parameters to achieve universal function approximation [9]. Therefore, network operators have to consider DNNs as large blackboxes [13, 14], which makes DL-based networking systems incomprehensible to debug and heavyweight to deploy (§2.1). As a result, network operators firmly hold

Z. Meng and M. Xu, *Latency Optimization in Interactive Multimedia Streaming*,
SpringerBriefs in Computer Science, https://doi.org/10.1007/978-981-97-6729-8_4

a general fear against using DL-based networking systems for interactive multimedia streaming and even other systems in practice.

Over the years, the machine learning community has developed several techniques for understanding the behaviors of DNNs in the scope of image recognition [15, 16] and language translation [17, 18]. These techniques focus on surgically monitoring the activation of neurons to determine the set of features that the neurons are sensitive to [16]. However, directly applying these techniques to DL-based networking systems is not suitable—network operators typically seek simple, deterministic control rules mapped from the input (e.g., scheduling packets with certain headers to a port) instead of nitpicking the operational details of DNNs. Besides, networking systems are diverse regarding their application settings and input data structure. The current DNN interpretation tools, designed primarily for well-structured vector inputs (e.g., images, sentences), are not sufficient across diverse networking systems. Therefore, a lightweight framework specifically tailored for interactive multimedia streaming is much needed.

In this chapter, our high-level design goal is to convert complicated interactive multimedia streaming systems into human-readable control policies so that network operators can easily debug, deploy, and ad-hoc adjust the systems. We develop Metis,[1] a general framework that provides interpretability and reduces the runtime overhead. To support a wide range of networking systems, Metis finds that a common feature shared by video streaming systems is that they are *local systems*, which collect information locally and make decisions for one instance only.

Specifically, we adopt a decision tree conversion method [19, 20] for local systems. The main observation behind the design choice is that existing heuristic interactive multimedia streaming systems are usually *rule-based* decision-making systems (§3.1) with a rather simple decision logic (e.g., buffer-based bitrate adaption (ABR) [21].) The conversion is built atop a teacher-student training process, where the complicated existing policy acts as the teacher and generates input-output samples to construct the student decision tree [20]. However, to match the performance with the original complicated policies such as DNNs, traditional decision tree algorithms [22] usually output an exceedingly large number of branches, which are effectively uninterpretable. We leverage two important observations to prune the branches down to a tractable number for network operators. First, sensible policies in the existing systems often unanimously output the same control action for a large part of the observed states. For example, any performant ABR policies [1] would keep a low bitrate when both the bandwidth and the playback buffer are low. By relying on the data generated by the teacher policy, the decision tree can easily cut down the decision space. Second, different input-output pairs have different contributions to the performance of a policy. We adopt a special resampling method [19] that allows the teacher policy to guide the decision tree to prioritize the actions leading to the best outcome. Empirically, the decision tree can generate human-readable interpretations and the performance degradation is within 2% of the original DNNs [23].

---

[1] Metis is a Greek deity that offers wisdom and consultation.

We generate interpretable policies for DL-based adaptive video streaming systems with Metis (§5.1). For example, we interpret the ABR policy of Pensieve [1] and recommend a new decision variable. We also present three use cases of Metis in the design, debugging, and deployment of DL-based networking systems. (i) Metis helps network operators to redesign the DNN structure of Pensieve with a quality of experience (QoE) improvement by 5.1%[2] on average (§5.2). (ii) Metis debugs the DNN in Pensieve and improves the average QoE by up to 4% with only decision trees (§5.3). (iii) Metis enables a lightweight Pensieve with shorter decision latency by 27× and lower resource consumption by up to 156× (§5.4).

2 Motivation

We motivate the design of Metis by analyzing (i) the drawbacks of current decision-making systems (§2.1), and (ii) why existing conversion methods are insufficient for decision-making systems (§2.2).

2.1 Drawbacks of Current Systems

The blackbox property of DNNs or ILP lacks interpretability for network operators. Without understanding why DNNs make decisions, network operators might not have enough confidence to adopt them in practice [14]. Moreover, as shown in Fig. 1, the blackbox property brings drawbacks to networking systems in debugging, online deployment, and ad-hoc adjustment due to the following reasons.

Heavyweight to deploy DNNs are known to be bulky on both resource consumption and decision latency [24]. Even with advanced hardware (e.g., GPU), DNNs may take tens of milliseconds for decision-making (§5.4). In contrast, networking systems,

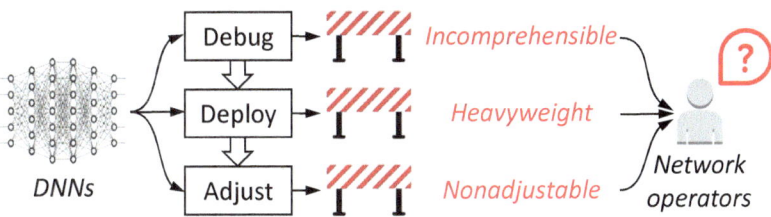

Fig. 1 DNNs create barriers for network operators in many stages of the development flow of networking systems

---

[2] Even a 1% improvement in QoE is significant to current Internet video providers (e.g., YouTube) considering the volume of videos [2].

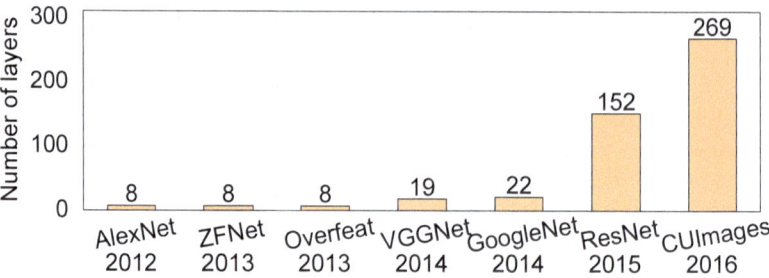

Fig. 2 The exponential growth of DNN complexity in ImageNet Challenge winners [28] (Figure adopted from [29])

especially local systems on end devices (e.g., mobile phones) or in-network devices (e.g., switches), are resource-limited and latency-sensitive [24]. For example, loading a DNN-based ABR algorithm on mobile clients increases the page load time by around 10 s [25, 26], which will make users leave the page. Existing systems usually provide "best-effort" services only and roll back to heuristics when resource and latency constraints can not be met [3], which degrades the performance of DNNs.

Incomprehensible structure DNNs could contain thousands to billions of neurons [12], making them incomprehensible for human network operators. Due to the complex structure of DNN, when DL-based networking systems fail to perform as expected, network operators will have difficulty in locating the erroneous component. Even after finding the sub-optimality in the design of DNN structures, network operators are challenged to redesign them for better performance. If network operators could trace the mapping function between inputs and outputs, it would be easier to debug and improve DL-based networking systems.

Nonadjustable policies The practical deployment of networking systems also requires ad-hoc adjustments or the addition of temporary features. For example, we could adjust the weights for different jobs in fair scheduling to catch up with the fluctuations in workloads [11]. However, the lack of interpretation makes it difficult for network operators to adjust the networking systems. Without understanding why DNNs make such decisions, arbitrary adjustments may lead to severe performance degradation. For example, when network operators want to manually reroute a flow away from a link without interpretations of decisions, network operators might not know how and where to accommodate that flow.

Discussions The application of DNNs in networking systems is still at a preliminary stage: DNNs in rate adaptation [1] and congestion control [27] are no way to compare with the recent large language model (LLM). As a comparison, a sharp increase in the number of DNN layers has been observed in other communities (Fig. 2). Recent LLMs even contain tens of billions of parameters [12]. Although we are not saying that the larger is the better, it is indisputable that larger DNNs will aggravate the problems and create barriers to deploying DL-based decision-making systems in practice.

2.2 Why Not Existing Interpretations?

For DL-based networking systems, existing interpretation methods [30, 31] are insufficient in the following aspects:

Different interpretation goal The question of *why a DNN makes a certain decision* may have answers from two angles. In the machine learning community, the answer could be understanding the *inner mechanism of ML models* (e.g., which neurons are activated for some particular input features) [15, 16]. It's like trying to understand how the brain works with surgery. In contrast, the expected answer from network operators is the *relationship between inputs and outputs* (e.g., which input features affect the decision) [14]. Network operators need a method to interpret the mapping between the input and output for DNNs.

Diverse networking systems DL-based networking systems have different application scenarios and are based on various DL approaches, such as feedforward neural network (FNN) [1], recurrent neural network (RNN) [32], and graph neural network (GNN) [11]. Therefore, interpreting diverse DL-based networking systems with one single interpretation method is insufficient. For example, LEMNA [33] could only interpret the behaviors of RNN and thus is not suitable for GNN-based networking systems [11]. In Metis, we observe that DL-based adaptive video streaming systems are actually local systems and develop corresponding techniques.

In response, to interpret DL-based networking systems, Metis introduces a decision tree-based method for DL-based adaptive video streaming systems.

3 Decision Tree Interpretations

In this section, we first describe the design choice for choosing decision trees in Metis (§3.1), and then explain the detailed methodology to convert the DNNs to decision trees (§3.2).

3.1 Design Choice: Decision Tree

As introduced in §1, Metis converts DNNs into simpler models based on interpretation methods. There are many candidate models, such as (super)linear regression [33, 34], decision trees [19, 20]. We refer the readers to [30, 31] for a comprehensive review.

In this chapter, we decide to convert DNNs to *decision trees* due to three reasons. First, the logical structure of decision trees resembles the policies made by networking systems, which are rule-based policies. For example, ABR algorithms depend on precomputed rules over buffer occupancy and predicted throughput [35, 36].

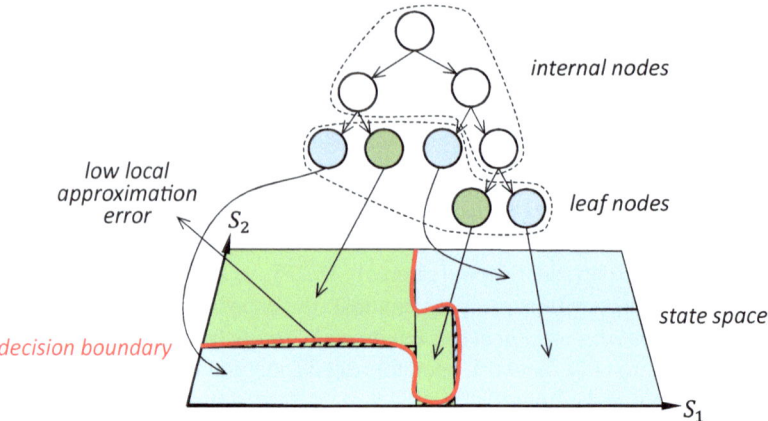

Fig. 3 An illustration of a decision tree approximating the original decision boundary

Second, as shown in Fig. 3, decision trees have rich expressiveness and high faithfulness because they are non-parametric and can represent very complex policies [37]. Third, decision trees are lightweight for networking systems, which will bring further benefits to resource consumption and decision latency (§5.4). Research efforts also interpret DNNs with programming language [38, 39]. However, designing different primitives for each networking system is time-consuming and inefficient.

We can interpret the results with interpretations in the form of decision trees since the decision-making process is transparent (§5.1). Also, we can debug the DNN models when they generate sub-optimal decisions (§5.3). Furthermore, since decision trees are much smaller in size and less expensive for computation, we could also deploy the decision trees online instead of deploying heavyweight DNN models. This will result in low decision-making latency and resource consumption (§5.4).

3.2 Conversion Methodology

To extract the decision tree from a finetuned DNN, we adopt a teacher-student training methodology proposed in [19]. Without teacher-student learning, one wrong prediction may drive the student off the teacher's trajectory in the state space. As shown in Fig. 4, a wrong decision may bring the decision tree into a region of inexperienced state space. The decision tree might thus make more mistakes since it has no prior knowledge about that region of state space. Those mistakes will further drive the decision tree off the trajectory and worsen the performance. In response, Metis continuously simulates the decision tree and lets the original ABR algorithm (teacher) correct the decisions made by that decision tree (student). The decision tree will gradually learn how to make decisions in the whole state space.

We reproduce key conversion steps for networking systems as follows:

Fig. 4 An illustration of how teachers correct students

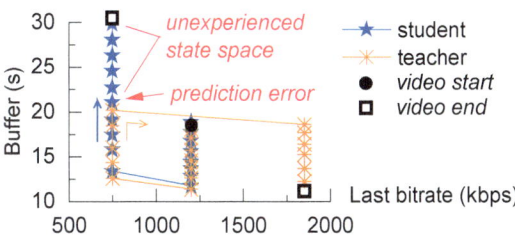

Step 1: Traces collection When training decision trees, obtaining an appropriate dataset from DNNs is important. Simply covering all possible (state, action) pairs is too costly and does not faithfully reflect the state distribution from the target policy. Thus, Metis follows the trajectories generated by the teacher DNNs. Moreover, networking systems are sequential decision processes, where each action has long-lasting effects on future states. Therefore, the decision tree can deviate significantly from the trajectories of DNNs due to imperfect conversion [19]. To make the converted policy more robust, we let the DNN policy take over the control on the deviated trajectory and re-collect (state, action) pair to refine the conversion training. We iterate the process until the deviation is confined (i.e., the converted policy closely tracks the DNN trajectory).

Step 2: Resampling Local systems usually optimize *policies* instead of independent actions [1, 3, 4]. In this case, different actions of networking systems may have different importance to the optimization goal. For example, an ABR algorithm downloading a huge chunk at an extremely low buffer will lead to a long stall, resulting in severe performance degradation. Meanwhile, downloading a little larger chunk when network condition and buffer are moderate will not have drastic effects. However, decision tree algorithms are designed to optimize the accuracy of a single action and treat all actions the same. Therefore, their optimization goals do not match. Existing DL-based decision-making systems adopt reinforcement learning (RL) to optimize the policy instead of single actions, where the *advantage* of each (state, action) represents the importance of the optimization goal. Therefore, we follow recent advances in converting DNNs in RL policies into decision trees [19] and resample $\mathcal{D}$ according to the advantage function. For each pair (s, a), the sampling probability $p(s, a)$ could be expressed as:

$$p(s, a) \propto \left(V^{(\pi^*)}(s) - \min_{a' \in A} Q^{(\pi^*)}(s, a') \right) \cdot \mathbb{1}\left((s, a) \in \mathcal{D} \right) \tag{1}$$

where $V(s)$ and $Q(s, a)$ are the value function and Q-function of RL [10]. Value function represents the expected total reward starting at state s and following the policy π. Q-function further specifies the next step action a. π^* is the DNN policy, and A is the action space. $\mathbb{1}(x)$ is the indicator function, which equals to 1 if and only if x is true. We then retrain the decision tree on the resampled dataset.

Step 3: Pruning As the size of the decision tree sometimes becomes much larger than network operators can understand, we adopt cost complexity pruning (CCP) [22] to reduce the number of branches according to the requirements of network operators. Compared with other pruning methods, CCP empirically achieves a smaller decision tree with a similar error rate [40]. At its core, CCP creates a cost function for the complexity of the pruned decision tree to balance accuracy and complexity. For Pensieve, the size of leaf nodes may be up to 1000 without pruning. With CCP, pruning the decision tree down to 200 leaf nodes only results in a performance degradation of less than 0.6% (§5.4).

Step 4: Deployment Finally, network operators could deploy the converted model online and enjoy both the performance improvement brought by deep learning and the interpretability provided by the converted model. Our evaluation shows that the performance degradation of decision trees is less than 2% for two DL-based networking systems (§5.4). We also present further benefits of converting DNNs of networking systems into decision trees (easy debugging and lightweight deployment) in §5.3 and §5.4.

4   Implementation

In current Internet video transmissions, each video consists of many *chunks* (a few seconds of playtime), and each chunk is encoded at multiple bitrates. Pensieve [1] is a deep RL-based ABR system to optimize bitrates with network observations such as past chunk throughput and buffer occupancy. We demonstrate the effect of the decision-making process with a series of experiments. We use the same video in Pensieve unless otherwise specified. The chunk size and bitrates of the video are respectively set to 4 s and {300, 750, 1200, 1850, 2850, 4300} kbps. Real-world network traces include 250 HSDPA traces [41] and 205 FCC traces [42]. We integrate DNNs into JavaScript with `tf.js` [43] to run Pensieve in the browser. We set up the same environment and QoE metric with Pensieve. We then implement Metis +Pensieve. We use the finetuned model provided by [1] to generate the decision tree. We use five baseline ABRs (BB [21], RB [1], Festive [44], BOLA [35], rMPC [36]) as Pensieve and migrate them into `dash.js` [45].

5   Experiments

In this section, we first empirically evaluate the interpretability of Metis with two types of DL-based networking systems. Subsequently, we showcase how Metis addresses the drawbacks of existing DL-based networking systems (§2.1). Overall, our experiments cover the following aspects:

- **System interpretations.** We demonstrate the effectiveness of Metis by presenting the interpretations of Pensieve with newly discovered knowledge (§5.1).
- **Guide for model design.** We present a case on how to improve the DNN structure of Pensieve for better performance based on the interpretations of Metis (§5.2).
- **Enabling debuggability.** With a use case of Pensieve, Metis debugs a problem and improves its performance by adjusting the structure of decision trees (§5.3).
- **Lightweight deployment.** Network operators could directly deploy the converted decision trees provided by Metis online and achieve benefits (§5.4).

5.1 System Interpretations

With Metis, we interpret the DNN policy learned by Pensieve. We present the top 4 layers of the decision tree of Metis +Pensieve in Fig. 5. The decision variables of each node include the last chunk bitrate (r^t), previous throughput (θ^t), buffer occupancy (B), and last chunk download time (T_t). Since we only present the top 4 layers of the decision tree, we represent the frequency of final decisions of each node with the color on the palette in Fig. 5.

From the interpretations in Fig. 5, we can know the reasons behind the superior performance of Pensieve in two directions.

(i) Discovering new knowledge. On the top two layers, Metis +Pensieve first classifies inputs into four branches based on the *last chunk bitrate*, which is different

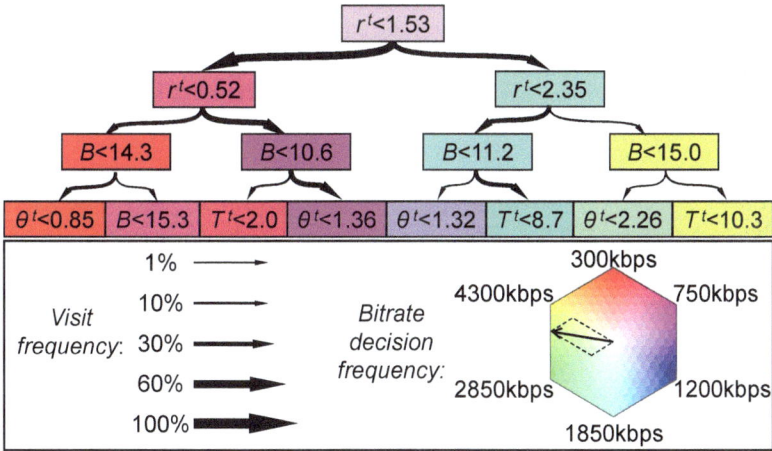

Fig. 5 Top 4 layers of the decision tree of Metis +Pensieve. The color represents the frequency of bitrate selections at that node. For example, the arrow in the palette represents that 67% states traversing a node with that color are finally decided as 4300kbps, and 33% states are 2850kbps. Better viewed with color

from existing methods. The information contained in the last bitrate choice affects the output QoE significantly. Based on this observation, we recommend that network operators improve ABR algorithms with a particular focus on the last chunk bitrate. We present a use case on how to utilize this observation to improve the DNN structure in §5.2.

(ii) Capturing existing heuristics. Similar to existing methods, Metis +Pensieve makes decisions based on buffer occupancy [21, 35] and predicted throughput [36, 45]. With the interpretations provided by Metis, network operators can understand how Pensieve makes decisions.

5.2   Guide for Model Design

We present a use case to demonstrate that the interpretations of Metis can help the design of the DNN structure of Pensieve. As interpreted in §5.1, Metis finds that Pensieve significantly relies on the last chunk bitrate (r^t) when making decisions. This indicates that r^t may contain important information for the optimization.

To utilize this observation, we modify the DNN structure of Pensieve to enlarge the influence of r^t on the output result. As shown in Fig. 6b, we directly concatenate the r^t to the output layer so that it can affect the prediction result more directly. Although the two DNN structures are mathematically equivalent, they will lead to different optimization performance and training efficiency due to the huge search space of DNNs [46]. After putting the significant feature nearer to the output layer (thus simplifying the relationship between the significant feature and results), the modified DNN will focus more on that significant feature.

We retrain the two DNN models on the same training and test sets and present the results in Fig. 7. From the curves of the original and modified models, we can see that the modification in Fig. 6 improves both the training speed and the final

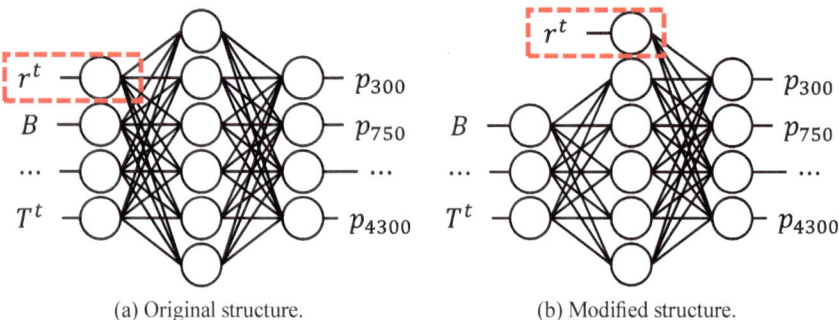

(a) Original structure.   (b) Modified structure.

Fig. 6 We modify the DNN structure of Pensieve based on the interpretations in §5.1. Although the two structures are equivalent in expressive ability, putting significant inputs near the output will make the DNN optimization easier and better

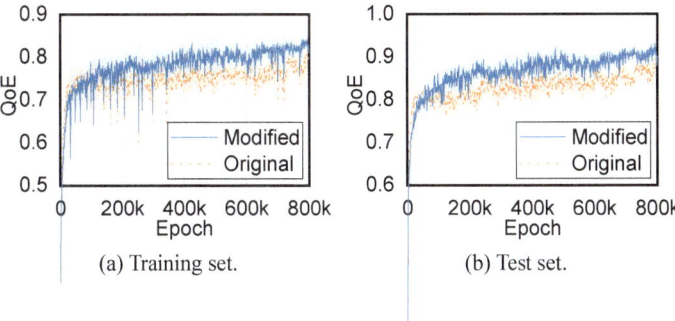

(a) Training set.

(b) Test set.

Fig. 7 The modification in Fig. 6 could improve both the QoE and the training efficiency. Shaded area spans ± std

QoE. For example, on the test set, the modified DNN achieves 5.1% higher QoE on average than the original DNN.[3] Considering the scale of views (millions of hours of video watched per day [47]) for video providers, even a small improvement in QoE is significant [2]. Moreover, the modified DNN can save 550k epochs on average to achieve the same QoE, which saves 23 h on our testbed.

5.3 Enabling Debuggability

When interpreting Pensieve, as also reported in [13], we observe that some bitrates are rarely selected by Pensieve. We emulate Pensieve on a set of links with fixed bandwidth ranging from 300kbps to 4500kbps. Among six bitrates from 300kbps to 4300kbps, two bitrates (1200kbps and 2850kbps) are rarely selected by Pensieve. The imbalance raises our interests since missing bitrates are *median* bitrates: the highest or lowest bitrates may not be selected due to network conditions, but not median ones. As shown in Fig. 8, 1200kbps and 2850kbps are not preferred by Pensieve. For example, on a fixed 3000kbps[4] link, the optimal decision of which should always be to select 2850kbps. However, in this case, only 0.4% of selections made by Pensieve are 2850kbps, while the remaining decisions are divided between 1850kbps and 4300kbps. As shown in Fig. 9, Pensieve oscillates between 1850kbps and 4300kbps, which is also mimicked by Metis +Pensieve. However, such a policy is sub-optimal. In contrast, other baselines learn the optimal selection policy and fix their decisions to 2850kbps, achieving a higher QoE. Similar observations can also be observed on a 1200kbps link.

Studying the raw outputs of Pensieve, we find that Pensieve does not have enough confidence in either choice and, therefore, oscillates between them. The probability of

---

[3] The offline optimality gap of Pensieve reported in [1] is 9.6%-14.3%.

[4] The goodput (bitrate) in this case is roughly 2850kbps.

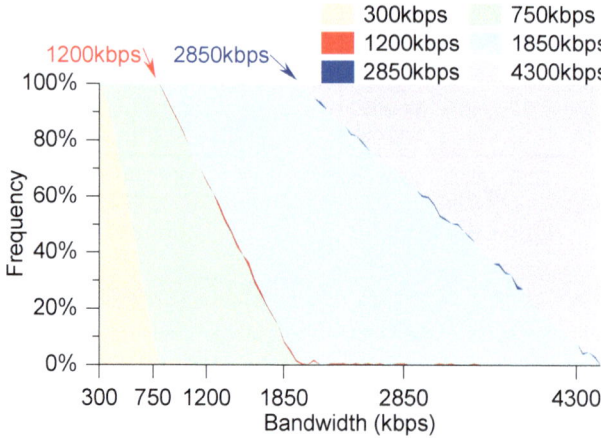

Fig. 8 On a set of fixed-bandwidth links when using Pensieve, 1200kbps and 2850kbps are not preferred. Better viewed in color

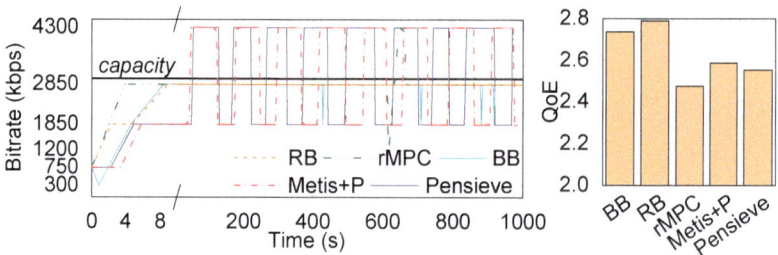

Fig. 9 On a 3000kbps link, BB, RB, and rMPC learn the optimal policy and converge to 2850kbps. Metis +Pensieve (Metis +P) and Pensieve oscillate between 1850kbps and 4300kbps, degrading the QoE. Better viewed in color

selecting the optimal bitrate is at a surprisingly low level. The training mechanism of Pensieve may cause this problem. At each step, the agent tries to *reinforce* particular actions that lead to larger rewards. In this case, when the agent discovers that four out of six actions can achieve a relatively good reward, it will keep reinforcing this discovery by continuously selecting those actions and finally abandoning the others. Making decisions with fewer actions brings higher confidence to the agent but also makes the agent converge to a local optimum in this case.

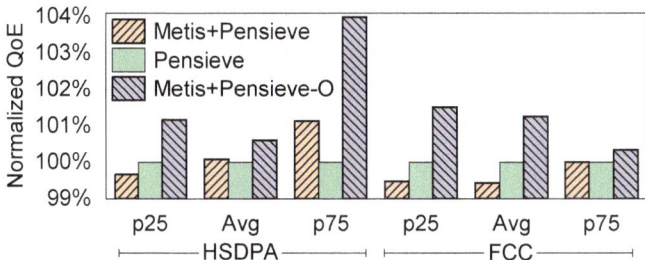

Fig. 10 When converting DNNs to decision trees in Metis, oversampling the missing bitrates (Metis +Pensieve-O) improves the QoE by around 1% on average compared to the original DNN in Pensieve. QoE is normalized by Pensieve

Beyond discovering the problem as [13], Metis can also help fix the problem. Without Metis, since Pensieve is designed based on RL, network operators do not have an explicit dataset of bitrates. Network operators may have to penalize the imbalance of bitrate in the reward and retrain the DNN model for hours to days without knowing whether the RL agent can learn to escape the local optimum itself. With Metis, the conversion from DNN to decision tree exposes an interface for network operators to debug the model. Since the dataset $\mathcal{D}$ to train the decision tree is highly *imbalanced*, as a straightforward solution, we oversample the missing bitrates to make sure their frequencies after sampling are around 1%. As shown in Fig. 10, the oversampled decision tree (Metis +Pensieve-O) outperforms DNNs by about 1% on average and 4% at the 75th percentile on HSDPA traces.

5.4 Lightweight Deployment

Decision trees provided by Metis are also lightweight to deploy. We first demonstrate that the performance degradation between the decision tree and the original DNN is negligible (less than 2%). Therefore, directly deploying decision trees of Pensieve online will reduce resource consumption and bring further performance benefits.

Resource consumption We evaluate the resource consumption (specifically, *page load time* and *memory consumption*) of Metis +Pensieve. To eliminate the influence of other modules in the DASH player, we compare these ABR algorithms with a fixed algorithm, which always selects the lowest bitrate.

For page load time, if the HTML page size is too large, users have to wait for a long time before the video starts to play. As shown in Fig. 11, Fixed, BB, RB, and BOLA have almost the same page size because of their simple processing logic. Pensieve increases the page size by 1370 KB since it needs to download the DNN model first. In contrast, Metis +Pensieve has a similar page size with the heuristics. When the goodput is 1200 kbps (the average bandwidth of Pensieve's evaluation traces), the *additional* page load time of ABR algorithms compared to fixed is

Fig. 11 Compared to the original Pensieve model, Metis +Pensieve could reduce both page size and JS memory

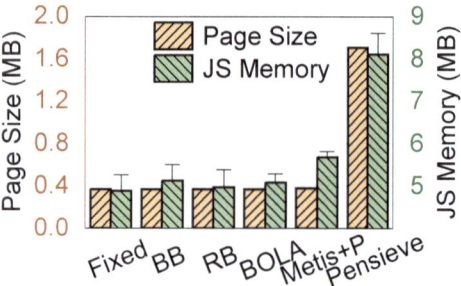

reduced by 156×: Pensieve introduces an additional page load time of 9.36 s, while Metis +Penseve only adds 60 ms.

We then measure the runtime memory and present the results in Fig. 11. Due to the complexity of forward propagation in neural networks, Pensieve consumes much more memory than other ABR algorithms. In contrast, the additional memory introduced by Metis +Pensieve is reduced by 4.0× on average and 6.6× on the peak, which is at the same level as other heuristics.

6 Discussion

This section discusses some design choices, the generalization ability, limitations, and potential future directions of Metis.

Why not directly train a decision tree? As shown in §5.4, converted decision trees exhibit comparable performance to larger models. However, *directly* training the simpler model from scratch makes it difficult to achieve the same performance. We hypothesize that the first reason is that decision trees are non-parametric models, which are not designed for continuous parameter updating and structure adjusting. Even with recent advances in decision tree adjusting [48], the efficient adjustment relies on a massive amount of training data. Another possible explanation behind this phenomenon is the *lottery ticket hypothesis* [49, 50]: training deep models is analogous to winning the lottery by buying a very large number of tickets (i.e., building a large neural network). However, we cannot know the winning ticket configuration in advance. Therefore, directly training a simpler model is similar to buying one lottery ticket only, which has little chance of achieving satisfying performance.

Can Metis interpret *all* types of networking systems? Admittedly, Metis cannot interpret all DL-based networking systems. For example, network intrusion detection systems (NIDSes) are used to detect malicious packets with regular expression matching on the packet payload [51]. Prior DL-based methods introduced RNN to improve the performance of NIDSes [32]. However, since RNN (and other DNNs with recurrent structures) fundamentally contains *implicit* memory units, decision trees cannot faithfully capture the policy with only *explicit* decision variables. In the future, we aim to combine Metis with recurrent units, e.g., employing recurrent decision trees [52].

How to interpret deeper DNNs? Although our evaluation shows satisfying performance on three DL-based networking systems, compared to the applications of DNNs in other communities (Fig. 2), those in networking systems are still at a preliminary stage: both Pensieve and AuTO have less than 10 hidden layers. Whether current approaches could scale to network systems with more complicated neural networks remains unknown. Nonetheless, on the one hand, Metis might be scalable to deeper neural networks because deeper neural networks (regardless of training difficulty) sometimes have the same level of expressiveness compared to shallower ones [53, 54]. On the other hand, as a preliminary attempt, we adopt the traditional CART algorithm in decision tree training. More optimized decision tree representations [55] with tree-based regularization [56] during the training process of DNNs might interpret the policies more faithfully.

Will the generalization ability of DNNs be impaired? Although the generalization ability of DNNs is still under exploration, it is indisputable that the generalization ability of DNNs roots in the massive amount of parameters [57]. Despite that Metis performs well in our experiment settings as demonstrated in §5, the generalization ability of interpretations still needs investigation. There are two ways to address the generalization ability of interpretations on different traces further. On the one hand, researchers can analyze the theoretic performance bounds of the interpretation [26]. On the other hand, network operators can deploy the interpretation results into the production environments and evaluate the online performance. We call on the community to devote more research efforts in this direction.

Will interpretations always be correct? Metis is designed to offer a sense of confidence by helping network operators understand (and further troubleshoot) DL-based networking systems. However, the interpretations themselves can also make mistakes. In fact, researchers have recently discovered attacks against the interpreting systems for image classification [58, 59]. Nonetheless, interpretations from our experiments are empirically sane (§5). Since the interpretations are concise and well understood, human operators could easily spot the rare case of erroneous interpretation.

7 Summary

In this chapter, we introduce Metis, a framework to convert heavyweight DL-based adaptive video streaming systems into lightweight decision trees for online deployment. The decision-making latency is also critical to the performance of interactive multimedia streaming systems.

Try it out!

The implementation codes of **Metis** are available at https://github.com/transys-project/metis.

References

1. Mao, H., Netravali, R., Alizadeh, M.: Neural adaptive video streaming with pensieve. In: Proc, ACM SIGCOMM (2017)
2. Mao, H., Chen, S., Dimmery, D., Singh, S., Blaisdell, D., Tian, Y., Alizadeh, M., Bakshy, E.: Real-world video adaptation with reinforcement learning. In: ICML Reinforcement Learning for Real Life Workshop (2019)
3. Chen, L., Lingys, J., Chen, K., Liu, F.: Auto: scaling deep reinforcement learning for datacenter-scale automatic traffic optimization. In: Proc, ACM SIGCOMM (2018)
4. Jay, N., Rotman, N., Godfrey, B., Schapira, M., Tamar, A.: A deep reinforcement learning perspective on internet congestion control. In: Proc, ICML (2019)
5. Rusek, K., Suárez-Varela, J., Mestres, A., Barlet-Ros, P., Cabellos-Aparicio, A.: Unveiling the potential of graph neural networks for network modeling and optimization in sdn. In: Proc, ACM SOSR (2019)
6. Xiao, Y., Zhang, Q., Liu, F., Wang, J., Zhao, M., Zhang, Z., Zhang, J.: Nfvdeep: Adaptive online service function chain deployment with deep reinforcement learning. In Proc, IEEE/ACM IWQoS (2019)
7. Zhang, M., Bai, J., Li, G., Meng, Z., Li, H., Hongxin, H., Mingwei, X.: When nfv meets ann: Rethinking elastic scaling for ann-based nfs. In Proc, IEEE ICNP (2019)
8. LeCun, Y., Bengio, Y., Hinton, G.: Deep learning. Nature **521**(7553), 436 (2015)
9. Leshno, M., Lin, V.Y., Pinkus, A., Schocken, S.: Multilayer feedforward networks with a nonpolynomial activation function can approximate any function. Neural Netw. **6**(6), 861–867 (1993)
10. Sutton, Richard S., Barto, Andrew G.: Reinforcement Learning (Second Edition): An Introduction. MIT press (2018)
11. Mao, H., Schwarzkopf, M., Venkatakrishnan, S. B., Meng, Z., Alizadeh, M.: Learning scheduling algorithms for data processing clusters. In: Proc, ACM SIGCOMM (2019)
12. Brown, T., Mann, B., Ryder, N., Subbiah, M., Kaplan, Jared D., Dhariwal, P., Neelakantan, A., Shyam, P., Sastry, G., Askell, A., Agarwal, S., Herbert-Voss, A., Krueger, G., Henighan, T., Child, R., Ramesh, A., Ziegler, D., Wu, J., Winter, C., Hesse, C., Chen, M., Sigler, E., Litwin, M., Gray, S., Chess, B., Clark, J., Berner, C., McCandlish, S., Radford, A., Sutskever, I., Amodei, D.: Language models are few-shot learners. In H. Larochelle, M. Ranzato, R. Hadsell, M.F. Balcan, and H. Lin, editors, Advances in Neural Information Processing Systems, volume 33, pages 1877–1901. Curran Associates, Inc. (2020)
13. Dethise, A., Canini, M., Kandula, S.: Cracking open the black box: What observations can tell us about reinforcement learning agents. In: Proc, ACM NetAI (2019)
14. Zheng, Y., Liu, Z., You, X., Yuedong, X., Jiang, J.: Demystifying deep learning in networking. In: Proc, ACM APNet (2018)
15. Zeiler, Matthew D., Fergus, R.: Visualizing and understanding convolutional networks. In: Proc. ECCV (2014)
16. Bau, D., Zhou, B., Khosla, A., Oliva, A., Torralba, A.: Network dissection: quantifying interpretability of deep visual representations. In Proc, IEEE CVPR (2017)

17. Toneva, M., Wehbe, L.: Interpreting and improving natural-language processing (in machines) with natural language-processing (in the brain). In Proc, NeurIPS (2019)
18. Ribeiro, M.T., Singh, S., Guestrin, C.: Semantically equivalent adversarial rules for debugging nlp models. In Proc, ACL (2018)
19. Bastani, O., Yewen, P., Solar-Lezama, A.: Verifiable reinforcement learning via policy extraction. In Proc, NeurIPS (2018)
20. Ross, S., Gordon, G., Bagnell, D.: A reduction of imitation learning and structured prediction to no-regret online learning. In Proc, AISTATS (2011)
21. Huang, T.-Y., Johari, R., McKeown, N., Trunnell, M., Watson, M.: A buffer-based approach to rate adaptation: Evidence from a large video streaming service. In Proc, ACM SIGCOMM (2014)
22. Friedman, Jerome H., Olshen, Richard A., Stone, Charles J., et al.: Classification and regression trees. Wadsworth & Brooks (1984)
23. Meng, Z., Wang, M., Bai, J., Mingwei, X., Mao, H., Hongxin, H.: Interpreting deep learning-based networking systems. In: Proc, ACM SIGCOMM (2020)
24. Huynh, Loc N., Lee, Y., Balan, R.K.: Deepmon: mobile gpu-based deep learning framework for continuous vision applications. In: Proc. ACM MobiSys (2017)
25. Meng, Z., Guo, Y., Shen, Y., Chen, J., Zhou, C., Wang, M., Zhang, J., Xu, M., Sun, C., Hu, H.: Practically deploying heavyweight adaptive bitrate algorithms with teacher-student learning. IEEE/ACM Trans. Netw. (2021)
26. Meng, Z., Chen, J., Guo, Y., Sun, C., Hongxin, H., Mingwei, X.: Pitree: Practical implementation of abr algorithms using decision trees. In Proc, ACM MM (2019)
27. Abbasloo, S., Yen, C.Y., Chao, H.J.: Classic meets modern: a pragmatic learning-based congestion control for the internet. In: Proc. ACM SIGCOMM (2020)
28. Deng, J., Dong, W., Socher, R., Li, L.-J., Li, K., Fei-Fei, L.: Imagenet: a large-scale hierarchical image database. In: Proc, IEEE CVPR (2009)
29. Pierre Ecarlat. Cnn - do we need to go deeper? https://medium.com/finc-engineering/cnn-do-we-need-to-go-deeper-afe1041e263e (2017)
30. Guidotti, R., Monreale, A., Ruggieri, S., Turini, F., Giannotti, F., Pedreschi, D.: A survey of methods for explaining black box models. ACM Comput. Surv. (CSUR) (2018)
31. Du, M., Liu, N., Hu, X.: Techniques for interpretable machine learning. Commun. ACM, pp. 68–77 (2020)
32. Yin, C., Zhu, Y., Fei, J., He, X.: A deep learning approach for intrusion detection using recurrent neural networks. IEEE Access, pp. 21954–21961 (2017)
33. Guo, W., Dongliang, M., Jun, X., Purui, S., Wang, G., Xing, X.: Lemna: explaining deep learning based security applications. In: Proc, ACM CCS (2018)
34. Ribeiro, M. T., Singh, S., Guestrin, C.: Why should i trust you?: explaining the predictions of any classifier. In: Proc. ACM KDD (2016)
35. Spiteri, K., Urgaonkar, R., Sitaraman, R.K.. Near-optimal bitrate adaptation for online videos. In: Proc. IEEE INFOCOM, Bola (2016)
36. Yin, X., Jindal, A., Sekar, V., Sinopoli, B.: A control-theoretic approach for dynamic adaptive video streaming over http. In: Proc, ACM SIGCOMM (2015)
37. Blockeel, H., De Raedt, L.: Top-down induction of first-order logical decision trees. Artif. Intell. **101**(1–2), 285–297 (1998)
38. Verma, A., Murali, V., Singh, R., Kohli, P., Chaudhuri, S.: Programmatically interpretable reinforcement learning. In: Proc, ICML (2018)
39. Zhu, H., Xiong, Z., Magill, S., Jagannathan, S.: An inductive synthesis framework for verifiable reinforcement learning. In: Proc, ACM PLDI (2019)
40. Mingers, J.: An empirical comparison of pruning methods for decision tree induction. Mach. Learn. **4**(2), 227–243 (1989)
41. Riiser, H., Vigmostad, P., Griwodz, C., Halvorsen, P.: Commute path bandwidth traces from 3g networks: Analysis and applications. In: Proc, ACM MMSys (2013)
42. Raw data - measuring broadband america. https://www.fcc.gov/reports-research/reports/measuring-broadband-america/raw-data-measuring-broadband-america-2016 (2016)

43. Smilkov, D., Thorat, N., Assogba, Y., Yuan, A., Kreeger, N., Yu, P., Zhang, K., Cai, S., Nielsen, E., Soergel, D., Bileschi, S., Terry, M., Nicholson, C., Gupta, Sandeep N., Sirajuddin, S., Sculley, D., Monga, R., Corrado, G., Viégas, Fernanda B., Wattenberg, M.: Tensorflow. js: machine learning for the web and beyond. In: Proc. SysML (2019)
44. Jiang, J., Sekar, V., Zhang, H.: Improving fairness, efficiency, and stability in http-based adaptive video streaming with festive. In Proc, ACM CoNEXT (2012)
45. Dash.js. https://github.com/Dash-Industry-Forum/dash.js (2018)
46. Elsken, T., Metzen, J. H., Hutter, F.: Neural architecture search: a survey. J. Mach. Learn. Res. (2019)
47. Wagner, K.: Facebook says video is huge – 100-million-hours-per-day huge. https://www.vox.com/2016/1/27/11589140/ (2016)
48. Manapragada, C., Webb, Geoffrey I., Salehi, M.: Extremely fast decision tree. In: Proc, ACM KDD (2018)
49. Frankle, J., Carbin, M.: The lottery ticket hypothesis: Finding sparse, trainable neural networks. In: Proc, ICLR (2019)
50. Yu, H., Edunov, S., Tian, Y., Morcos, Ari S.: Playing the lottery with rewards and multiple languages: lottery tickets in rl and nlp. In: Proc. ICLR (2020)
51. Modi, C., Patel, D., Borisaniya, B., Patel, H., Patel, A., Rajarajan, M.: A survey of intrusion detection techniques in cloud. Elsevier J. Netw. Comput. Appl. pp. 42–57 (2013)
52. Chen, J., Le, H.M., Carr, P., Yue, Y., Little, J.J.: Learning online smooth predictors for realtime camera planning using recurrent decision trees. In: Proc. IEEE CVPR (2016)
53. Ba, J., Caruana, R.: Do deep nets really need to be deep? In Proc, NIPS (2014)
54. Hanin, B., Rolnick, D.: Complexity of linear regions in deep networks. In: Proc, ICML (2019)
55. Narodytska, N., Ignatiev, A., Pereira, F., Marques-Silva, J., IS RAS.: Learning optimal decision trees with sat. In: Proc. IJCAI (2018)
56. Mike, W.: Michael C Hughes, Sonali Parbhoo, Maurizio Zazzi, Volker Roth, and Finale Doshi-Velez. Tree regularization of deep models for interpretability. In: Proc. AAAI, Beyond sparsity (2018)
57. Novak, R., Bahri, Y., Abolafia, D. A., Pennington, J., Sohl-Dickstein, J.: Sensitivity and generalization in neural networks: an empirical study. In: Proc. ICLR (2018)
58. Zhang, X., Wang, N., Ji, S., Shen, H., Wang, T.: Interpretable deep learning under fire. In: Proc, USENIX Security (2020)
59. Heo, J., Joo, S., Moon, T.: Fooling neural network interpretations via adversarial model manipulation. In: Proc, NeurIPS (2019)

Chapter 5
Application Layer on Data Path: Adaptive Frame Rate

Abstract This chapter explores the application layer of data paths with a focus on Adaptive Frame-Rate (AFR) in interactive multimedia streaming. We examine key components such as codec optimization, adaptive bitrate algorithms, and multimedia transmission protocols. By analyzing existing solutions and their limitations, we highlight the importance of managing decoder queue delays to meet the stringent latency requirements of ultra-high-definition, high frame-rate applications like cloud gaming. Our findings underscore the need for AFR techniques to ensure smooth, real-time user experiences by dynamically adjusting frame rates based on network conditions and client capabilities.

Keywords Interactive multimedia streaming · Video decoder · Frame-rate control · Application layer latency

1 Application Layer on Data Path

Interactive multimedia streaming applications mainly include the following key components: First, when a video source generates an image, the encoder must encode the image into a video stream. For example, video conference images are obtained from the user's camera, while cloud gaming and virtual reality images are rendered by the GPU. All of these require the original video to be encoded before it can be transmitted. Second, during the video encoding process, the encoding parameters (mainly the bitrate) need to be adjusted in real time based on network conditions. For instance, when the network conditions improve, the encoder can increase the encoding bitrate to deliver clearer video content to the user. Similarly, when network conditions worsen, the encoder will reduce the bitrate to ensure that the user can at least see smooth content. Third, once the content is ready, the sender needs to send it using a protocol specific to the application for better content management (Table 1).

There has been an increasing amount of work in recent years on multimedia transmission, particularly in the application layer and in conjunction with application design. We will introduce these efforts in the following sections.

Z. Meng and M. Xu, *Latency Optimization in Interactive Multimedia Streaming*,
SpringerBriefs in Computer Science, https://doi.org/10.1007/978-981-97-6729-8_5

Table 1 Related work of interactive multimedia streaming on the application layer

Academic/industry proposals	Solution	Main approach
Swift (NSDI'22) [1]CGEncoder (MMSys'20) [2]VP9 (Google'13) [3]	Real-time Video Codec	Ensure content decoding in weak network conditions through updated codec design
BB (SIGCOMM'14) [4] Pensieve (SIGCOMM'17) [5] Puffer (NSDI'20) [6]	Adaptive Bitrate Algorithm	Adapt bitrate to bandwidth, reducing buffering
RTP/RTCP (RFC8888) [7] RTSP (RFC7826) [8] DTP (ICNP'21) [9]	Multimedia Transmission Protocol	Protocol design to convey necessary application information
AFR (NSDI'23) [10]	Frame rate adaptation	Adapt the frame rate to network and client loads

1.1   Codec Optimization

The history of codec development is long, and its range of applications is extensive. The main principle of video encoding is to exploit video content's temporal and spatial correlations, significantly compressing the content through differential value storage and other methods to save bandwidth costs. The most widely used codec today is H.264 [11]. In recent years, codec optimization efforts have mainly focused on optimizing the codec performance and tailoring the codec design to specific application scenarios. In terms of codec performance optimization, a new H.265 codec mechanism has been introduced in recent years [12], which can save considerable bandwidth costs at the same level of clarity. However, due to various issues, such as patent rights, its deployment is far from ideal compared to H.264. Recently, researchers have also been promoting the standardization and demonstration of H.266 codec applications. In the field of interactive multimedia streaming, the VP9 codec promoted and deployed by Google is currently the most widely used [3]. It is now included in the WebRTC real-time audio and video transmission framework and can be easily used by developers.

In addition, other research efforts have focused on optimizing other application metrics, such as image or video quality (e.g., SSIM [13] or PSNR [14]). For example, Alfalfa [15] specifically optimizes the multi-threaded parallelism of a large number of users during the transcoding process of interactive multimedia streaming. Salsify [16] further makes the encoder aware of network conditions and reserves space for network adjustments. The most recent work, Swift [1], uses neural network techniques to further optimize the encoding efficiency and processing latency of the codec, allowing users to use virtual reality (VR) and other technologies more smoothly. CGEncoder [2] combines the characteristics of cloud gaming and other gaming applications, first analyzing the specific needs of game users-the user experience of game users may not necessarily be entirely consistent with objective indicators of clarity such as PSNR or SSIM. Based on this, it further designs a codec mechanism to make the codec more suitable for cloud gaming scenarios. The work mentioned above is orthogonal to the interaction latency (per-frame latency) that we are concerned with; they focus on video clarity while we focus on the potential interaction lag that users may experience. Therefore, the optimizations for clarity mentioned above can coexist with the latency optimizations of this work.

At the same time, the biggest problem in designing codecs is the issue of deployability. Video decoding has a strong demand for real-time performance: when one video frame is played, the next frame should have been decoded and ready to play to avoid user perception of buffering. However, encoding and decoding involve a large number of mathematical operations, which are extremely resource-intensive within the CPU. As a result, existing solutions usually have dedicated encoding and decoding chips within the CPU or graphics card to speed up the decoding process. However, these hardware decoding chips may not necessarily support the emerging encoding and decoding mechanisms mentioned above. In fact, many works themselves mention one of their major shortcomings as not being supported by existing hardware. Therefore, although the H.264 encoding mechanism has been proposed for more than 20 years, it remains the most widely used encoding and decoding mechanism.

1.2 Adaptive Bitrate Optimization

As mentioned in the introduction, adaptive bitrate is one of the essential components of existing multimedia transmission mechanisms. Its primary function is to modify the encoding bitrate of the encoder according to the fluctuations in network conditions, ensuring that the encoder's bitrate does not exceed the network's carrying capacity. Adaptive bitrate algorithms have been proposed with the birth of interactive multimedia streaming. In the past decade, a typical algorithm is the Buffer-based algorithm proposed by Netflix [4]. It innovatively suggests adjusting the multimedia bitrate in the network by estimating the client-side buffer status in on-demand multimedia videos. When the client buffer is low, the risk of the client stuttering increases, and the encoding bitrate needs to be reduced to deliver new content to the client as soon as possible. When the client buffer is high, the encoder can try to explore a higher encoding bitrate to provide better image quality for the user. In this direction, there are also algorithms like BOLA [17], which make decisions based on buffer occupancy but can also perform theoretical analysis based on Lyapunov stability. BOLA is currently the default adaptive bitrate algorithm for the widely used on-demand streaming media framework dash.js. After that, further improvements and enhancements have been made with algorithms like BOLA-E [18], further optimizing buffer-based methods.

In addition, there are sending rate estimation algorithms, such as PANDA [19] and Squad [20], which are similar to congestion control and estimate the most suitable video bitrate for transmission based on network conditions. In parallel, many adaptive rate control algorithms are based on buffer and network status. For example, some researchers have proposed using integer programming to systematically model the adaptive bitrate problem and proposed the RobustMPC algorithm [21] for optimization and solving, obtaining the most suitable bitrate decision for current transmission. In recent years, machine learning algorithms have been used to optimize adaptive bitrate algorithms. Pensieve [5], presented at the SIGCOMM 2017 conference, is the first work to use deep neural networks to optimize adaptive bitrate selection. It uses deep reinforcement learning to model the adaptive bitrate problem and designs corresponding state spaces, action spaces, and reward functions, using a series of algorithms to optimize adaptive bitrate algorithms. Subsequently, further optimizations have been made to neural network structure and optimization methods in works like HotDASH [22] to enhance user experience. This area of work has been a hot topic in academia in recent years. However, there is still a significant gap between current algorithms [5, 21] and theoretically optimal analyses. Therefore, we believe there is still much room for improvement. For example, the academic community has continuously held competitions to seek better QoE algorithms [23]. In summary, to achieve better performance, continuously optimized methods have been (and will continue to be) proposed [23].

In this chapter, we will present a work that is more concerned with reducing the delays inherent in the application layer. Therefore, existing algorithms in the architecture proposed in Chap. 1 do not target delay jitter or extreme tail latency optimization.

1.3 Multimedia Transmission Protocol Design

Another important research work in recent years is the design of new multimedia transmission protocols. Application layer protocols are indispensable in the Internet architecture. On top of transport layer protocols, appropriate application layer protocols are needed to ensure the correct transmission of content. The most widely used protocol recently is the RTP/RTCP protocol [7]. RTP and RTCP are a pair of UDP-based protocols, where RTP sends packets from the server to the client to transmit video content, making it a data path protocol; RTCP is responsible for feeding back network status, video status, and other state information from the client to the server, making it a control path protocol. RTCP constructs Sender Reports (SR) and Receiver Reports (RR) to report sender and receiver information. RTCP also constructs NACK (Negative Acknowledgment) and TWCC (Transport-wide Congestion Control) messages to report packet loss and delay situations to the sender. The sender can selectively decide whether to retransmit certain packets. In this case, such a UDP-based application layer protocol can essentially achieve almost reliable transmission. Both the open-source framework WebRTC [24] and industrial solutions like Zoom [25] or Google Meet [26] use this protocol or its variants for transmission.

Historically, protocols like RTSP [8] for multimedia transmission applications have also existed. These protocols are based on reliable transmission protocols like TCP, eliminating the need to ensure transmission reliability at the application layer.

Recently, some researchers have noticed the latency-sensitive requirements of emerging applications and proposed deadline-aware transport protocols (DTP) [9, 27] that carry deadline information for corresponding data packets in the protocol design. In this case, both network devices and receivers can schedule data packets more reasonably based on the deadline information of data packets, maximizing the satisfaction of application requirements.

In contrast, this chapter does not propose a new application layer protocol but seeks reliable low latency on the existing framework. This is because, from a deployability perspective, we want our solution to be as compatible and coexistent with existing frameworks as possible, making it valuable for practical applications. At the same time, existing protocol designs do not explicitly address application latency requirements. The work at the application layer in this chapter can coexist with almost all common application layer protocols.

2 Adaptive Frame Rate

To achieve a satisfactory user experience, high-quality real-time communication (RTC) applications need to stream with ultra-high definition (UHD), high frame rate (HFR), and reduced delays (§3). For example, cloud gaming services deliver content with a resolution of $\geq 1080p$ [28] and frame rate of 60fps [29] while requiring a tail end-to-end delay of less than 100ms [30]. Streaming like this significantly improves users' experience and enables new applications.

This chapter presents a view that, in addition to modulating bitrate to match network capacity, an interactive multimedia streaming system must regulate the queuing at the decoder queue. For traditional standard quality RTC, the time required to decode a frame is much shorter than the interarrival time of frames. Thus, the decoder queue is not a bottleneck, and a traditional RTC service only needs to adjust the bitrate to match the network bandwidth. However, in interactive multimedia streaming, the high frame rate reduces the time between the arrival of frames at the client, while the high resolution increases the decoding delay for each frame. At the decoder queue, the frame arrival rate frequently exceeds the departure rate, leading to a long queue, as shown in Fig. 1. The video delivery is required to not only adapt the bitrate to the network bandwidth but also coordinate with the decoder queue capacity. From measurements of a production cloud gaming service, we find that video delivery without coordinating the queue capacity could introduce a nonnegligible queuing delay at the client-side decoder queue. Moreover, such a queuing delay accounts for a large proportion of delayed frames in satisfying the much tighter delay requirement of interactive multimedia streaming, especially when the network delay has been reduced with recent infrastructure developments (e.g., edge computing [31]). According to our measurements, among all frames with a total round-trip delay of $>100ms$, 57% of them have been delayed at the decoder queue for $>50ms$ (§4.1). Our survey finds that the future demands of UHD and HFR video will further exacerbate the problem, even with the evolution of decoding hardware (§4.1). Therefore,

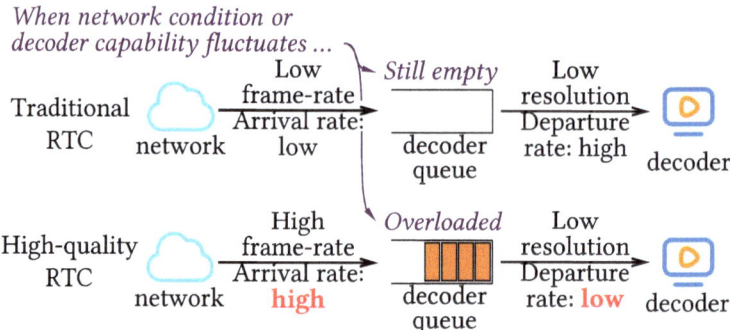

Fig. 1 Comparison of the decoder queue between traditional and interactive multimedia streaming applications. Due to the high frame rate and resolution, when network condition or decoder capability fluctuates, interactive multimedia streaming applications may overload decoder queues, leading to high delay at the tail

for interactive multimedia streaming, to reduce the end-to-end delay, it is essential to reduce the queuing delay at the decoder.

Not all interventions are effective at regulating the queuing at the decoder queue (§4.2). For instance, the decoding delay is not affected much by bitrate. It is affected by resolution, but adjusting the resolution requires the client to request a new keyframe. This consumes bandwidth and incurs several extra frame intervals of delay. Discarding a frame at the client also requires a new keyframe, which incurs the same cost. Hence, we introduce an *adaptive frame rate (AFR)* controller, which controls the frame rate at the *encoder*. Reducing the frame rate gives the decoder more time to process frames. Hence, it is effective at reducing the queue length. Further, edge streaming services offer short RTTs, which means the control loop to adjust the encoder's frame rate is short.

Note that there have been previous efforts to adapt the frame rate (e.g., CU-SeeMe [32] decades ago). However, the development of decoding hardware has made it redundant in the recent decade, and traditional RTC has mostly bottlenecked the network. In this chapter, we show how interactive multimedia streaming, with UHD resolution, HFR, and stringent delay requirements, has changed this. We further improve upon these proposals in two ways. First, existing control mechanisms are based on delay or queue length [16, 33, 34], which are slow to react since they need to wait for the queue to build up. AFR instead relies on the arrival and service processes in addition to the queue length to adjust the frame rate. Second, not all increases in decode queuing delay need to reduce the frame rate. For instance, when queueing delay increases due to a transient burst of arriving packets. Hence, AFR uses two control loops that adjust the frame rate at different time scales.

3 Background: High-Quality RTC

High-quality RTC applications are attracting attention from the industry and academia. A series of interactive multimedia streaming products have been released recently, including cloud gaming [28, 35, 36], virtual reality (VR) [37–39], and 4K videoconferencing [40]. For example, by generating high-quality content and streaming to the user via the Internet, users can enjoy better video quality with low-cost devices. Specifically, we again remind the readers that interactive multimedia streaming has the following features that stand out from traditional RTC applications:

- *High frame rate.* Traditional RTC usually delivers content with a low frame rate (LFR) of 24 fps [41]. However, interactive multimedia streaming requires a frame rate of up to 60 fps, some of which even require a frame rate of 240 fps [42].
- *High resolution.* Most existing RTC applications are delivered at SD resolutions by default (e.g., 360p for Google Meet [43]). In contrast, interactive multimedia streaming applications require a resolution of 1080p to 4K or higher [44].
- *Stringent delay requirement.* Furthermore, interactive multimedia streaming applications also have stringent latency requirements. For example, videoconferencing requires an interaction delay of 150 ms [41] and gaming for 100 ms [30].

Existing delivery pipeline To better understand the bottleneck of interactive multimedia streaming, we present the key components of the existing RTC delivery pipeline in Fig. 2. First, the video encoder captures the contents generated from video sources (e.g., gaming applications [31, 45]) and encodes them into video frames. Then, encoded frames are sent over the network from the streaming server to user clients. After that, on the client side, upon receiving new frames from the network, the decoder will decode those frames. Finally, decoded video frames will be displayed on users' displays.

Optimization goal: low tail delay With the intelligence from each community, the delay of each component has been intensively optimized in recent research efforts. To reduce the network delay, existing providers either deploy stream servers at the edge [31, 46], introduce low-latency congestion controllers [47, 48], or suggest users

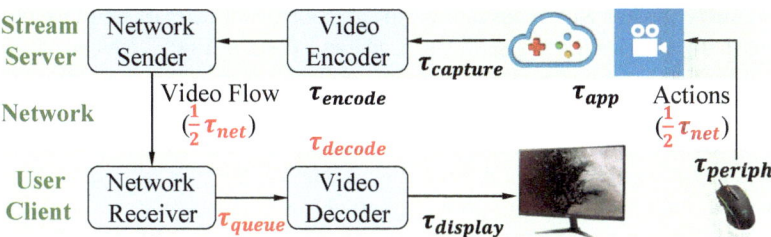

Fig. 2 A general delivery pipeline of interactive multimedia streaming. We highlight the major contributing components in the tail end-to-end delay of interactive multimedia streaming according to our measurements in red

use wired connections. For example, recent measurements unveil that cloud gaming services could deliver the RTC streams with an average round-trip network delay of 20ms [31, 49]. Similarly, streaming encoders are optimized for low latency to satisfy the stringent delay requirements in interactive multimedia streaming services [16, 50, 51].

Meanwhile, optimizing the *tail* performance is also critical for the user's experience for interactive multimedia streaming [52]. The increase in tail delay will result in frame stuttering or freezing, degrading the user's experience. Quality of experience assessment frameworks in video streaming usually individually calculate the stuttering time as a penalty to the user's experience [23, 53]. Considering the high frame rate of interactive multimedia streaming, further tails of 99th or 99.9th percentiles need to be focused on. For example, at the frame rate of 60fps, even the 99.9th percentile delay could happen every 16 s. Especially for applications such as cloud gaming, such a delay might lead to the loss of the game (e.g., stalls when the gamer is discovered by the opponent in a shooting game) [30, 54]. Therefore, controlling the tail delay and reducing frame stutters for interactive multimedia streaming is essential.

4   Motivations and Challenges

This section explains the formulation of drastic queuing delay in interactive multimedia streaming (§4.1). We then present our thinking over the design choice of adjusting frame rate (§4.2). We further analyze the unique challenges of effectively achieving an ultra-short queue (§4.3).

4.1   Motivation: Drastic Queuing Delay

Observation: decoder queuing delay is a critical contributor to the total delay at the tail We profile the delay of each frame at each stage in the delivery pipeline in Fig. 2. We measure one cloud gaming service for a month in 2021, containing tens of thousands of users with thousands of different CPU and GPU models. We present release dates and benchmark scores of CPU and GPU in Fig. 3. Unless otherwise specified, all measurements in this chapter are analyzed from this dataset.

According to the measurements, among all components in the pipeline, the network, queuing (at the decoder queue), and decoding delay are >10ms at the 99th percentile. We highlight them in red in Fig. 2. The tail delay at the application and encoding is light since they are processed on commercial servers, which are stable compared to networks and heterogeneous clients. Therefore, the following discussion focuses on the network, queuing, and decoding delay.

We investigate how these three components contribute to the increase in total delay at the tail. For each frame, we denote N, Q, D, and T as the network, queuing,

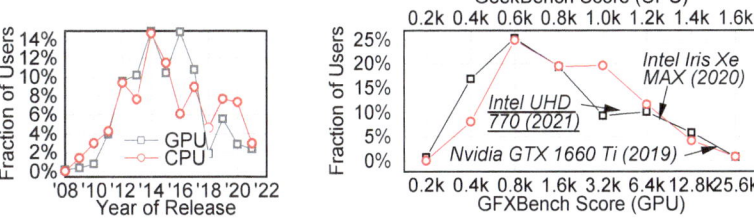

Fig. 3 Release year (**left figure**) and benchmark score (**right figure**) distributions of user devices in production. We use the single-core score in GeekBench [55] for the CPU benchmark and Aztec Ruins Normal Tier score in GFXBench [56] for the GPU benchmark

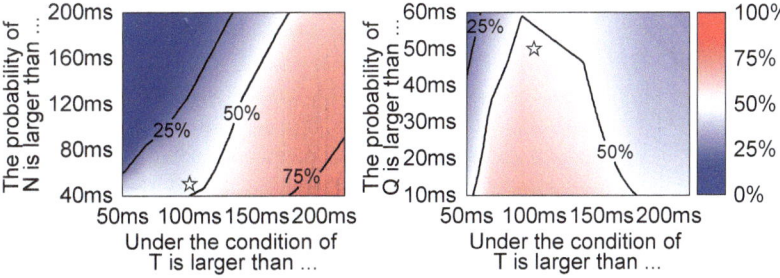

Fig. 4 While network delay should usually be blamed when the total delay is above 200ms (**left figure**), queuing delay plays a dominant role among all frames with a total delay of more than 100ms (**right figure**). The color indicates the conditional probability $P(X > X_{th}|T > T_{th})$ for $X \in \{N, Q\}$. Stars denote X_{th} =50ms, Please generate equation alttext for inline equation MathID8 T_{th}=100ms

decoding, and total end-to-end delay. We then calculate the conditional probability of $P(X > X_{th}|T > T_{th})$ for each $X \in \{Q, D, C\}$ from our measurements, where X_{th} and T_{th} are thresholds for statistics. A high conditional probability suggests that the component is more likely the cause of $T > T_{th}$. We calculate the conditional probability with different thresholds and present the network and queuing delay results in Fig. 4.

As we can see, when analyzing the root causes of frames with T>200ms for traditional RTC services, network delay has a high probability (shaded red) to be blamed. However, when analyzing the frames with T>100ms for interactive multimedia streaming, queuing delay dominates the increase of total delay. Our measurements show that among all frames with an end-to-end total delay of more than 100ms, queuing delay increase happens more frequently than all other component delays: 57% of them have a queuing delay of more than 50ms (stars in Fig. 4). Considering the stringent delay requirement of ∼100ms for interactive multimedia streaming, the increase in queuing delay plays a dominant role.

Root cause: The UHD resolution and HFR jointly contribute to the increase in queuing delay Compared to LFR streaming, HFR increases the arrival rate of the decoder queue by reducing the interarrival time between frames. Also, UHD decreases the departure rate compared to SD streaming by increasing the decoding delay of each frame.

Specifically, we illustrate how the frame rate and resolution could affect the load of the decoder queue by presenting the 99%ile queue utilization in Fig. 5. We scale the distribution of interarrival time and decoding delay from our measurements to other frame rates and resolutions. As we can see, for traditional RTC services (the down-left corner), due to their low frame rates and resolutions, the decoder queue still has a utilization of $\rho \ll 1$ at the tail. However, for interactive multimedia streaming applications (the up-right corner), the decoder queue would be heavily loaded, leading to a drastic queuing delay.

The issue is the inconsistency of the decoder's performance *on average* and *at tail*. In fact, many of the hardware decoders that we measured claim to support UHD and HFR videos (e.g., Nvidia GTX series). However, according to our measurement, supporting UHD and HFR does not really mean *consistently* supporting. For example, the decoding delay can fluctuate due to numerous reasons, including overheating at the client [57], CPU scheduling, and prediction errors [58], all of which are difficult to control for an application. From our measurement with devices in production, the decoding delay is 18ms at the 99th percentile, even with hardware acceleration. Note that at the frame rate of 60fps, the interarrival time between frames is 16.7ms, resulting in a heavily loaded decoder queue at the tail.

Further analysis of the necessity and sufficiency between the increase of other components and total delay figures out that the minor fluctuation of decoding delay leads to the increase of queueing delay. From the queuing theory, when the queue is heavily loaded, the queuing delay will drastically increase [59]. This is because while the decoding delay continuously fluctuates, the queuing delay accumulates all the fluctuations of precedent frames. Especially in heavy traffic, a minor fluctuation of the decoding delay could result in a magnitude increase in queuing delay. We refer the readers to [59] for more theoretical analysis. Illustratively, we present a trace from our production service in Fig. 6. In the trace, the interarrival time is 16ms, and the decoding delay is 18ms, while the queuing delay is 54ms on average. The

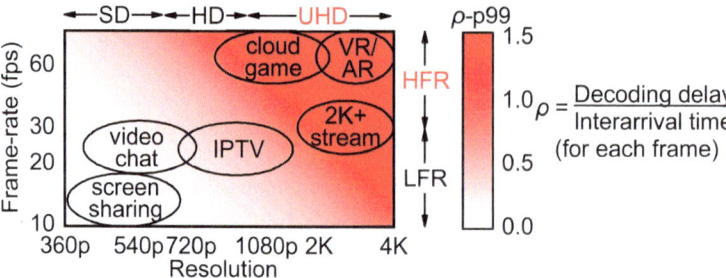

Fig. 5 Illustration of the 99th percentile of the utilization ρ of the decoder queue. For interactive multimedia streaming applications (in the top-right corner), the decoder queue is heavily loaded at the tail (shaded red), resulting in an increase in queuing delay at the tail

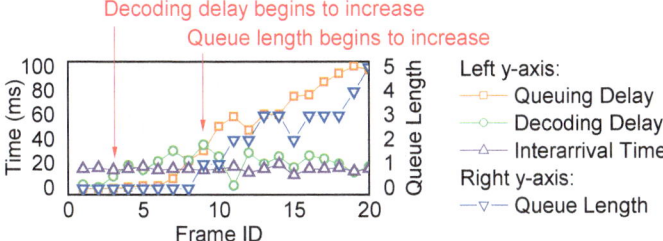

Fig. 6 A trace for the accumulation of decoder queue as an illustrative example

continual increase of the decoding delay, although not much by magnitude (18ms) and not long by duration (20 frames, approximately 0.3 s), leads to a drastic queuing delay. If such a trace happens with a probability of 1%, we will have a 99th percentile decoding delay of 18 ms and a 99th percentile queuing delay of 55 ms. In this case, the tail queuing delay is much higher than the decoding delay, which also contributes to more than half of the end-to-end stutters as analyzed in §4.1.

Trend: hardware decoders cannot keep pace with the increasing demands of UHD and HFR video User demands for video have increased sharply, as shown in Fig. 7. For example, YouTube's highest supported resolution and frame rate have increased from 360p@30fps (7Mpx/s) in 2005 to 8K@60fps in 2015 (2Gpx/s), doubling every 14 months on average. Emerging services at 16K [44, 61] or 240fps [42] further indicate the future demands of UHD and HFR streaming.

However, the decoding speed of the hardware is not increasing as fast. We summarize the decoding speed of state-of-the-art video decoders from recent academic chapters [61–66]. As shown in Fig. 8, the decoding speed of the state-of-the-art decoding hardware doubles only approximately every 27 months (blue dotted line). Meanwhile, we also calculate the required decoding speed from the existing demands

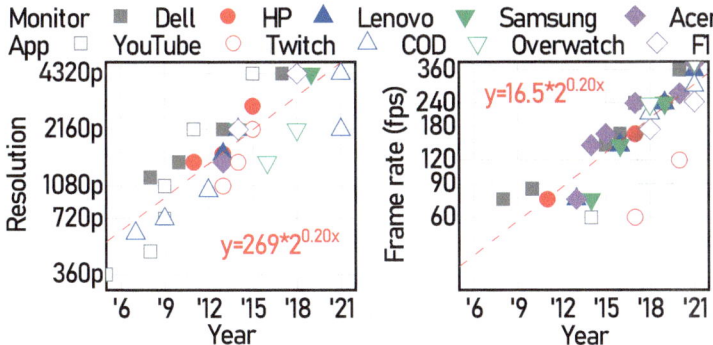

Fig. 7 Maximum supported resolution and frame rate for the top 5 monitor vendors, two streaming platforms (YouTube and Twitch) and three games (Call-of-duty, Overwatch, and F1) [60]

Fig. 8 Decoding speed of existing hardware and required decoding speed from demands. Note that the required decoding speed from demands is the frame rate times the *square* of resolution times the aspect ratio

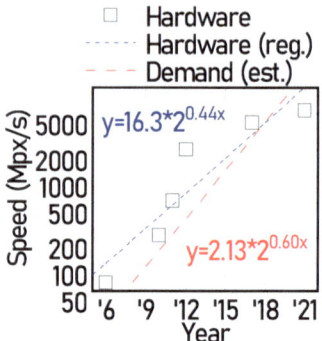

of videos by multiplying the estimated resolution and frame rate from Fig. 7 and plot the estimation in red in Fig. 8. The required decoding speed from demands doubling every 20 months (red dashed line) increases much faster than the development of decoding hardware (blue dotted line), indicating the continuous incapability of decoding hardware for UHD and HFR videos.

In addition to the state-of-the-art hardware, there are still a considerable number of low-end and mid-end devices in our users. Even in the same generation, user devices could also be very heterogeneous. For example, in Fig. 3, notice that the performance of Intel Iris Xe is $2\times$ better than Intel UHD 770 even though the latter is more recent. Thus, there is heterogeneity in user devices even in the same generation. Moreover, new video codecs (e.g., H.265), although with a higher compression ratio, even slow down the decoding speed by up to 60% [3, 67, 68]. In this case, the mismatch between the decoder and UHD and HFR videos will further exacerbate, making the queuing delay at the tail a lasting issue.

4.2 Choice: Controlling Proper Parameters

We motivate the need to adjust the frame rate. For an encoder, there are three parameters that could be independently set, including the frame rate, bit rate, and resolution. The encoder will automatically optimize other parameters (e.g., quantization parameters) based on current contents to achieve the target frame rate, bit rate, and resolution. We refer readers to [69] for more details on video codec.

We first analyze how these parameters could affect the delay of different components. When the bitrate increases, the network delay will increase due to the congestion. When the resolution increases, since the decoder needs to decode frames with larger pixels, it needs a longer time to decode. The queuing delay depends on the enqueue rate (i.e., frame rate) and the dequeue rate (i.e., decoding delay). In contrast, for example, if the bitrate decreases, yet the resolution is kept the same, the decoding delay for each frame will hardly decrease due to the hardware design of the codec.

Thus, relying on the total delay (e.g., Salsify [16]) would lead to ambiguity in taking effective actions to reduce the delay.

Therefore, we need to control the respective parameters to reduce individual delays. In response, we adjust the frame rate to control the queuing delay for interactive multimedia streaming. When the fluctuations of the decoder and network result in an increase in queuing delay, it is essential to adjust the encoding parameters to reduce the queuing delay. In this case, after collecting measurements from the client and network, the server's encoder could adjust the frame rate for the following frames accordingly. We could dynamically specify certain timestamps where new frames are encoded.

In summary, adjusting the resolution or dropping frames is impractical due to the significant overhead of bandwidth. Statically choosing the frame rate based on the client model is also insufficient due to the fluctuation of decoding delay in the runtime. Moreover, since applications have limited control over users' systems, it is also impractical to control the user's system (e.g., pinning the application to a CPU core) for a large-scale production-level service [70]. In terms of frame rate adaption, note that there are previous efforts in the adaption of frame rate (e.g., CU-SeeMe [32] decades ago). However, as we discussed in §4.1, with the increase in resolution and frame rate, and the stringent delay requirements, we need to reemphasize the significance of adapting the frame rate now. We also show that it is timely enough to control the frame rate over the Internet.

4.3 Challenges

Achieving an ultra-short queue To achieve an ultra-short queuing delay for the decoder queue, picking the appropriate indicator to inform the controller when it needs to take action is challenging. Existing signals (queue length [33] or queuing delay [16, 34]) fail to achieve an ultra-short queuing delay. Since the accumulation of the decoder queue is the consequence of the fluctuation of the arrival or departure process, both the queue length and queuing delay can only be observed when the queue has already been built up. For the example in Fig. 6, while the decoding delay starts to increase at the 3rd frame, a nonzero queue length can only be observed by the 9th frame.

We want to capture the *earliest signal* to perceive the potential queuing delay. Therefore, instead of measuring the queuing delay, we want to predictively estimate the potential increase of queuing delay. For example, inspired by recent advances in congestion control [71, 72], a straightforward way is to measure the dequeue rate of the decoder queue to estimate the potential increase of the queuing delay.

However, in terms of tails, the arrival process is also fluctuating, which could also lead to an increase in queuing delays. For example, the network delay might increase by ten times at the 99th percentile than the median [48]. In response, to precisely avoid queue accumulation, we extend the designs of [71, 72]: AFR comprehensively

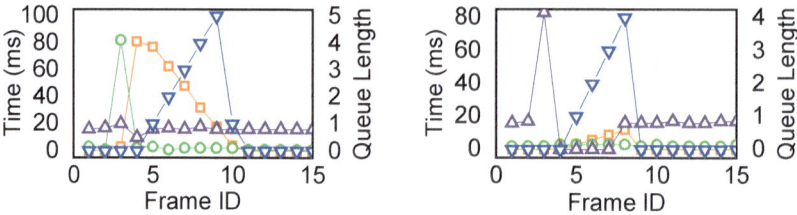

Fig. 9 Traces of transient fluctuations of the decoder queue from online traces: (**left figure**) stalled decoder services; and (**right figure**) bursty network arrivals. Legends are the same as Fig. 6.

measures the arrival and departure process and controls the queuing delay based on queuing theory. We introduce the design in §5.2.

Handling various events Furthermore, the reason behind the formulation of the decoder queue in interactive multimedia streaming is complex. As we introduced in §4.1, the stationary degradation of decoding capacity could lead to the accumulation of the decoder queue, e.g., the traces in Fig. 6. Besides, the decoder queue could also be accumulated due to transient contingencies. For example, from our experiences in production, the decoder might contingently experience a sudden decoding lag of ~100 milliseconds (e.g., the 3rd frame in the left figure of Fig. 9). The sudden interference in wireless channels might also lead to the bursty arrival of several frames (e.g., the 4th to 8th frames in the right figure of Fig. 9). In both cases, the decoder queue will be accumulated. Since these transient fluctuations happen suddenly, it is challenging for the controller to react by measuring enqueue and dequeue rates.

Thus, AFR differentiates the causes of queue accumulation and reacts respectively to fluctuations at different time scales. We design a stationary controller to avoid queue accumulation in heavy traffic (§5.2) and a transient controller to reduce the queuing delay in contingencies (§5.3).

5 AFR Design

We first analyze the overall workflow of AFR in §5.1 and then present the two controllers of AFR (§5.2, §5.3).

5.1 Workflow Overview

The workflow of AFR is presented in Algorithm 3. Specifically, the stationary controller (§5.2) maintains the queue around an ultra-short target based on the dynamics of enqueue and dequeue processes. By measuring the statistics of both processes, AFR calculates the expectation of the queuing delay based on queuing theory. The frame rate can, therefore, be optimized towards a given queuing delay target (line

---

Algorithm 3: Hierarchical AFR control

Input: Enqueue process $\{A_n\}$, dequeue process $\{S_n\}$, queue states Q. (A_n denotes the interarrival times, and S_n denotes the decoding delays of frames $\{n\}$.)
Output: Target frame rate f.
1 $f_0 = \text{StationaryController}(\{A_n\}, \{S_n\})$
2 $\alpha = \text{TransientController}(Q)$
3 $f = \alpha f_1$

---

1). The transient controller observes the queue states Q (queue length and queuing delay) and calculates the discounting factor $\alpha \leqslant 1$ (line 2) to further decrease the frame rate when the queue formulates. The final frame rate is the stationary frame rate f_0 discounted by α (line 3). In this case, AFR can react to various scenarios of queue accumulation.

5.2 Stationary Controller

As introduced above, we measure the arrival and service processes and control the expected queuing delay. Specifically, we use the Kingman formula as an approximation of the expectation of queuing delay. Kingman formula is a widely adopted approximation formula of queuing delay [73] for G/G/1 queues. Compared to other approximation methods, in this chapter, we adopt the Kingman formula to estimate the queuing delay since its estimation is from *both arrival and departure processes* without relying on queue states, which could provide the earliest signal for the potential queuing delay. According to the Kingman formula, the expectation of queuing delay τ_{queue} follows:

$$\mathbb{E}\left(\tau_{\text{queue}}\right) \approx \left(\frac{\rho}{1-\rho}\right) \left(\frac{c_a^2 + c_s^2}{2}\right) \mu_s \tag{1}$$

where

$$c_a = \sigma_a/\mu_a, \quad c_s = \sigma_s/\mu_s, \quad \rho = \mu_a/\mu_s \tag{2}$$

(μ_a, σ_a) and (μ_s, σ_s) are the mean and standard deviation of the arrival and service processes:

$$\mu_a = \mathbb{E}\{A_n\}, \sigma_a = \sqrt{\text{var}(A_n)}, \mu_s = \mathbb{E}\{S_n\}, \sigma_s = \sqrt{\text{var}(S_n)} \tag{3}$$

From Eq. (1), the queuing delay is related to the following factors:

- Queue utilization ρ. The queuing delay will increase when the queue is overloaded ($\rho \to 1$). The current frame rate and decoding delay determine the queue utilization.

- Arrival and service fluctuations c_a and c_s. When the arrival or the service processes fluctuate, the queuing delay will also increase.
- Service time μ_s. Finally, the queuing delay scales with the average decoding delay.

Therefore, we control the expected queuing delay by controlling the right-hand side (RHS) of Eq. (1). We set $\mathbb{E}\{\tau_{\text{queue}}\}$ to a predefined queuing delay target W_0. Consequently, the target frame rate f_0 could be calculated as:

$$f_0 = \rho/\mu_s = 1 \bigg/ \left(\mu_s \cdot \left(1 + \frac{\mu_s}{W_0} \cdot \frac{c_a^2 + c_s^2}{2} \right) \right) \tag{4}$$

Discussion: Approximation method The AFR mechanism supports any approximation formula by design. There are other research efforts to control the queue. For example, recent efforts in congestion control [71, 72] directly set the target utilization (e.g., setting $\rho = 0.95$) and calculate the enqueue rate. In this chapter, we adopt the Kingman formula to capture *both the arrival and departure processes*, as discussed in §4.3.

Measurements of queuing dynamics According to Eq. (4), we need to measure the mean and variance of the arrival and service processes. Similar to the RTT measurements in TCP [74], we adopt the exponentially weighted moving average (EWMA) and exponentially weighted moving variance (EWMV) to estimate the μ_s, σ_s, μ_a, σ_a in Eqs. (1) and (2).

$$\hat{\mu}_n = \xi_\mu x_n + \left(1 - \xi_\mu \right) \hat{\mu}_{n-1}$$
$$\hat{\sigma}_n = \sqrt{\xi_\sigma \left(x_n - \hat{\mu}_n \right)^2 + (1 - \xi_\sigma) \hat{\sigma}_{n-1}^2} \tag{5}$$

where x_n denotes interarrival time A_n or service time S_n. $\hat{\mu}_n$ and $\hat{\sigma}_n$ are the EWMA and EWMV. ξ_μ and ξ_σ are the discounting factors for the measurement of mean and standard deviation, trading off between precision and sensitivity.

However, due to bursty arrival or stalled services (§5.1), both the arrival and service processes could have significantly deviated value. For example, the 3rd frame in Fig. 9 has a decoding time of 82ms while other frames are below 4ms. Such outliers will significantly deviate the estimation of stationary statistics for a long period. In fact, as we discussed in §5.1, these contingent events are designed to be handled by the transient controller. Therefore, we need to filter those outliers out to precisely estimate the stationary status of arrival and service processes. Due to the highly skewed distribution of decoding delay, existing outlier removal mechanisms based on standard deviation (e.g., the three-σ rule [75, 76]) suffer from differentiating stationary state transitions from outliers.

To capture the transitions of the status of decoders while eliminating the influence of the contingent outliers, we introduce an outlier removal mechanism based on prior knowledge from measurements in production. The key intuition is that *decoding delay differences* $(S_n - S_{n-1})$ are related to the probability of being outliers. For example, an increase of 20 ms in the decoding delay is probably the transition between stationary states (Fig. 6). However, a sudden increase of 80 ms in decoding delay is likely to indicate that decoding delay is an outlier, which is usually the scenario of contingent stalls in Fig. 9. This is because commercial decoders are usually able to decode frames at the frame rate of 24fps on average. According to our measurements, when the decoding delay difference is above 50 ms, the possibility of being an outlier for that frame is 95%. Thus, we remove frames with a decoding delay difference of >50ms in the stationary controller and leave the control of those frames to the transient controller.

We further characterize our observation based on measurements in production. As shown in Fig. 10, we quantify the outlier with *reflection ratio r*, which illustrates the recovery of decoding delay before and after the potential outlier. The numerator is the difference between the current decoding delay (τ_0) and the average decoding delay of the previous 10 frames ($\tau_{-10:-1}$), and the denominator is the difference between τ_0 and future decoding delay. For outliers of contingent stalled service (e.g., the 3rd frame in the decoder example in Fig. 9), their reflection ratios would approach -1. This is because previous frames and subsequent frames have similar decoding delays, while the outlier has a much higher decoding delay ($\tau_0 \gg \tau_{-10:-1} \approx \tau_{1:10}$).

We then plot the relationship between the difference of decoding delay ($\tau_0 - \tau_{-1}$) and the average reflection ratio (r) of all frames with the same difference from our measurements in Fig. 10. When the decoding time difference is larger than 50 ms (marked with a red arrow), the average reflection ratio is less than -0.95, indicating that most frames in this scenario are outliers. Therefore, the stationary controller in AFR does not calculate the frames with a decoding delay difference larger than 50 ms.

Convergence time analysis To help operators better understand the behavior of the stationary controller, we investigate the convergence of the stationary controller during state transitions of the service process. We want to answer the following question: During the transition from stationary state (μ_1, σ_1) to (μ_2, σ_2), how long will the stationary controller take to converge to the new frame rate and drain the potential accumulation of the queue due to the transition?

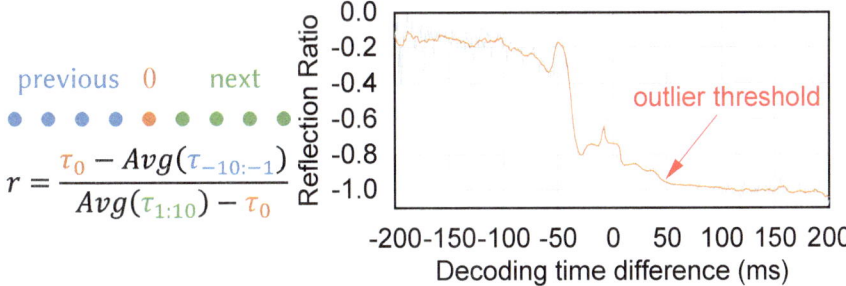

Fig. 10 Reflection in outlier removal, with the illustration (**left**) and the measurement results (**right**). This figure presents the frequency of frames with $r \in [\frac{1}{C}, C]$

We outline the main conclusion here and leave the detailed analysis to [10]. When the control loop (round-trip delay) of AFR is τ frames, the convergence time T_0 is bounded w.r.t. τ and W_0, and is acceptable for most scenarios. For example, when the average control loop of AFR is the interarrival time of one frame ($\tau=1$), and $W_0=2\text{ms}$, the stationary controller could converge to the new stationary state within 2 frames.

5.3 *Transient Controller*

The transient controller is designed to handle the contingent queue accumulations (§5.1). Therefore, we need to first understand how we should react to these queue contingencies.

Understanding queue contingencies As shown in Fig. 9, both stalled decoder services and bursty network arrivals will cause a sudden increase in queue length. We illustrate the enqueue and dequeue events of two contingencies in Fig. 11. In the example of bursty network arrival in Fig. 11, 5 frames arrive at the client together within 4ms, resulting in a queue length of 4 when the 5th frame arrives and observes, as illustrated with the L_Q (blue arrow). In the example of stalled decoder service, the decoder takes 80ms to decode the 0th frame when queued frames cannot be dequeued to the decoder. Therefore, upon the arrival of the 5th frame, a queue length of 4 is observed.

However, the bursty network arrivals and stalled decoder services should be handled separately. In the scenario of bursty network arrivals, the bottleneck of total delay is still in the network due to its long network delay. As long as the decoder is functional, even if multiple frames arrive at the queue simultaneously, they can be processed efficiently (the left figure in Fig. 11). In this case, the queue will be drained in a short time, and we do not need to reduce the frame rate. In contrast, the stalled decoder service will drastically increase the queuing delay of subsequent frames and

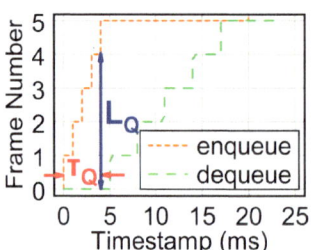 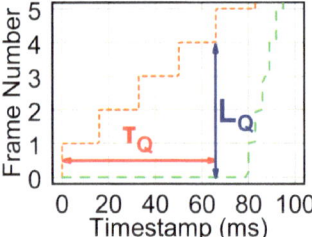

Fig. 11 Differences between bursty network arrivals (**left**) and stalled decoder (**right**) services. The y-axis is the accumulated enqueue/dequeue frames. For example, the enqueue curve in the left figure increases from 1 to 2 at 1ms, indicating that frame #2 enqueues at 1ms

Fig. 12 Decoder queue that stores all frames

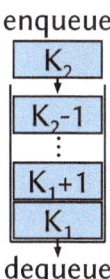

enqueue

dequeue

needs adaption (the right figure in Fig. 11). Thus, we need to differentiate between the two scenarios.

Since both scenarios result in an increase in queue length, they cannot be effectively differentiated by queue length only. Our insight is that we can differentiate them with the sojourn time of the first frame in the queue. As shown in Fig. 12, at the arrival of frame K_2, the sojourn time τ_Q of the first frame K_1 and queue length L_Q observed by K_2 are:

$$\tau_Q = t_{enq}^{(K_2)} - t_{enq}^{(K_1)}, \qquad L_Q = K_2 - K_1 \tag{6}$$

where $t_{enq}^{(i)}$ is the enqueue timestamp of frame #i, and frame #K_1 is the frame at the head of the queue. For bursty network arrivals, since frames arrive at the decoder queue simultaneously, when the last frame of the burst arrives, the first frame has only been queued for a short time. For example, τ_Q in the example of bursty network arrivals is 4ms (marked red). In contrast, for stalled decoder service, the head frame has been blocked for a long time, leading to a high τ_Q of 66ms in Fig. 11. Therefore, we use τ_Q to adjust the frame rate in the transient controller.

Feedback control For the transient controller, the design space is to find out a mapping between the discounting factor α and the queuing delay τ_Q. Since the transient controller is designed to reduce the frame rate based on the results of the stationary controller, the possible range of α satisfies:

$$\frac{f_{min}}{f_{max}} = \alpha_{min} \leqslant \alpha \leqslant 1 \tag{7}$$

where f_{min} and f_{max} are the lower and upper bounds for the frame rate required by the application. Since longer τ_Q indicates a more severe load of the queue, the discounting factor should decrease with the increase of τ_Q. Besides, the α-τ_Q mapping should also have the following properties:

First, avoid overreactions. As we discussed above, for bursty network arrivals, τ_Q will also slightly increase due to the volumetric arrived frames. However, since such a transient queue accumulation will be cleared quickly as long as the decoder is functional (Fig. 9), we should not decrease the frame rate. Therefore, we need to introduce an upper reservoir (as shown in Fig. 13) to avoid overreactions. In the upper reservoir, when a nonzero but small τ_Q is observed ($0 \leqslant \tau_Q \leqslant Q_1$), the transient controller will not decrease the frame rate. The reservoir threshold Q_1 should be set based on measurements. We measure the observed L_Q and τ_Q from frames and present the results in Fig. 14. Peaks near the left axis (marked by red dashed arrows) represent frames with a long L_Q yet a short τ_Q due to the bursty network arrivals. Therefore, we set Q_1 to filter out those bursty arrival-related peaks (e.g., $Q_1 = 14$ ms in our measurement, the red line in Fig. 14).

Second, respond quickly. Due to the stringent delay requirements of interactive multimedia streaming applications, a long queuing delay will drastically degrade the users' experiences. Therefore, we need to control the slope of the mapping in Fig. 13 to effectively reduce the queuing delay. Since α is lower bounded, we could control the slope of the mapping by introducing a *lower reservoir*, as shown in Fig. 13. We set Q_2 as the maximum tolerable queueing delay:

$$Q_2 = \max\left(Q_1, \text{Deadline} - \tau_{\text{network}} - \tau_{\text{decode}}\right) \tag{8}$$

where τ_{network} is the round-trip network delay, and τ_{decode} is the decoding delay μ_s. *Deadline* is the requirement for the total delay of the application. Based on users' experiences in the human–machine interaction and our operational experiences, we set *Deadline* to 100ms in our deployments [30].

Fig. 13 Illustrations of the α-τ_Q mapping of the transient controller

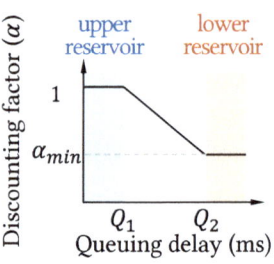

Fig. 14 Measurements of the L_Q-τ_Q frequencies of the transient controller. A series of linearly distributed dark blue clusters in Fig. 14 indicate that L_Q and τ_Q are linearly correlated

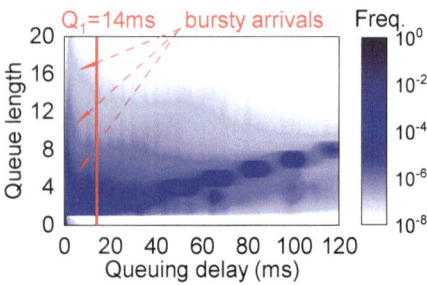

6 Implementation

This book also provides an implementation of AFR with a frame-level trace-driven simulator for the convenience of users. To faithfully compare and replay the traces for different queue control algorithms, we design a simple simulation environment that models the dynamics of RTC. The simulator maintains the decoder queue and replays the traces collected from online services, where the traces contain the decoding delay, network delay, original queuing delay, and arrival timestamp for each frame. Specifically, frames arrive at the decoder queue according to timestamps in traces, wait in the decoder queue for dequeuing, and are decoded according to decoding delays in traces. To avoid frequently sending frame rate adjustment requests to the servers, frame rates are quantized at the level of 5fps, which is also followed by our online deployment. We implement the potential interference from CPU time-slicing: since the fetching of frames to decoders depends on the CPU, there are possible cases where fetching the frame from the queue to the decoder needs waiting to be scheduled by the CPU by up to several milliseconds [77]. Therefore, we further profile such a delay in the traces and introduce the scheduling waiting time in our simulator. We also implement the response time of the encoder between the new frame rate actions and new frames generated with the updated frame rate, according to the input traces.

7 Summary

In this chapter, we propose AFR to reduce the queuing delay of the decoder queue for interactive multimedia streaming by dynamically adjusting the frame rate. AFR introduces a stationary controller and a transient controller to mitigate the stationary heavy traffic and contingent arrivals and services respectively.

Try it out!
The implementation codes of AFR are available at https://github.com/transys-project/afr.

References

1. Dasari, M., Kahatapitiya, K., Das, S.R., Balasubramanian, A., Samaras, D.: Swift: Adaptive video streaming with layered neural codecs. In Proc, USENIX NSDI (2022)
2. Zadtootaghaj, S., Schmidt, S., Sabet, S. S., Möller, S., Griwodz, C.: Quality estimation models for gaming video streaming services using perceptual video quality dimensions. In: Proc. ACM MMSys (2020)
3. Bultje, Ronald S.: The world's fastest vp9 decoder: ffvp9. https://blogs.gnome.org/rbultje/2014/02/22/the-worlds-fastest-vp9-decoder-ffvp9/ (2014)

4. Huang, T.-Y., Johari, R., McKeown, N., Trunnell, M., Watson, M.: A buffer-based approach to rate adaptation: evidence from a large video streaming service. In Proc, ACM SIGCOMM (2014)
5. Mao, H., Netravali, R., Alizadeh, M.: Neural adaptive video streaming with pensieve. In Proc, ACM SIGCOMM (2017)
6. Yan, Francis Y., Ayers, H., Zhu, C., Fouladi, S., Hong, J., Zhang, K., Levis, P., Winstein, K.: Learning in situ: a randomized experiment in video streaming. In: Proc. USENIX NSDI (2020)
7. Sarker, Z., Perkins, C., Singh, V., Ramalho, M.: Rtp control protocol (rtcp) feedback for congestion control. IETF RFC 8888 (2021)
8. Schulzrinne, H., Rao, A., Lanphier, R., Westerlund, M., Stiemerling, M.: Real-time streaming protocol version 2.0. IETF RFC 7826 (2016)
9. Zhang, L., Cui, Y., Pan, J., Jiang, Y.: Deadline-aware transmission control for real-time video streaming. In Proc, IEEE ICNP (2021)
10. Meng, Z., Wang, T., Shen, Y., Wang, B., Mingwei, X., Han, R., Liu, H., Arun, V., Hongxin, H., Wei, X.: Enabling high quality real-time communications with adaptive frame-rate. In Proc, USENIX NSDI (2023)
11. x264 - wikipedia. https://en.wikipedia.org/wiki/X264
12. x265 - wikipedia. https://en.wikipedia.org/wiki/X265
13. Wang, Z., Bovik, A.C., Sheikh, H.R., Simoncelli, E.P.: Image quality assessment: from error visibility to structural similarity. IEEE Trans. Image Proc. (2004)
14. Peak signal-to-noise ratio - wikipedia. https://en.wikipedia.org/wiki/Peak_signal-to-noise_ratio, 2020
15. Fouladi, S., Wahby, R.S., Shacklett, B., Balasubramaniam, K.V., Zeng, W., Bhalerao, R., Sivaraman, A., Porter, G., Winstein, K.: Encoding, fast and slow: low-latency video processing using thousands of tiny threads. In: Proc. USENIX NSDI (2017)
16. Fouladi, S., Emmons, J., Orbay, E., Wu, C., Wahby, R. S., Winstein, K.: Salsify: low-latency network video through tighter integration between a video codec and a transport protocol. In: Proc. USENIX NSDI (2018)
17. Spiteri, K., Urgaonkar, R., Sitaraman, Ramesh K.: Near-optimal bitrate adaptation for online videos. In Proc. IEEE INFOCOM, Bola (2016)
18. Spiteri, K., Sitaraman, R., Sparacio, D.: From theory to practice: improving bitrate adaptation in the dash reference player. In Proc, ACM MMSys (2018)
19. Li, Z., Zhu, X., Gahm, J., Pan, R., Hu, H., Begen, A.C., Oran, D.: Probe and adapt: rate adaptation for http video streaming at scale. IEEE J. Sel. Areas Commun., pp. 719–733 (2014)
20. Wang, C., Rizk, A., Zink, M.: Squad: a spectrum-based quality adaptation for dynamic adaptive streaming over http. In: Proc. ACM MMSys pp. 1–12 (2016)
21. Yin, X., Jindal, A., Sekar, V., Sinopoli, B.: A control-theoretic approach for dynamic adaptive video streaming over http. In Proc, ACM SIGCOMM (2015)
22. Sengupta, S., Ganguly, N., Chakraborty, S., De, P.: Hotdash: hotspot aware adaptive video streaming using deep reinforcement learning. In: Proc. IEEE ICNP pp. 165–175 (2018)
23. Yi, G., Yang, D., Bentaleb, A., Li, W., Li, Y., Zheng, K., Liu, J., Ooi, W.T., Cui, Y.: The acm multimedia 2019 live video streaming grand challenge. In: Proc. ACM Multimedia, pp. 2622–2626 (2019)
24. Psa: Webrtc m88 release notes. https://groups.google.com/g/discuss-webrtc/c/A0FjOcTW2c0/m/UAv-veyPCAAJ, 2020
25. Marczak, B., Scott-Railton, J.: Move fast and roll your own crypto: a quick look at the confidentiality of zoom meetings - the citizen lab. https://citizenlab.ca/2020/04/move-fast-roll-your-own-crypto-a-quick-look-at-the-confidentiality-of-zoom-meetings/ (2020)
26. brianhu. Google meet troubleshooting playbook - network and hardware troubleshooting. https://www.googlecloudcommunity.com/gc/Workspace-Product-Articles/Google-Meet-Troubleshooting-Playbook-Network-and-Hardware/ta-p/165810, 2021

27. Shi, H., Cui, Y., Qian, F., Yuming, H.: Dtp: Deadline-aware transport protocol. In Proc, APNet (2019)

28. Stadia - one place for all the ways we play. https://stadia.google.com/, 2020

29. OPG609. List of 60fps games playable on ps5. https://www.reddit.com/r/PS5/comments/kiuh2t/list_of_60fps_games_playable_on_ps5/, 2020

30. Ivkovic, Z., Stavness, I., Gutwin, C., Sutcliffe, S.: Quantifying and mitigating the negative effects of local latencies on aiming in 3d shooter games. In: Proc. ACM CHI pp. 135–144 (2015)

31. China Mobile and ZTE. Powered by sa: 5g mec-based cloud game innovation practice. GSMA 5G Case Studies (https://www.gsma.com/futurenetworks/wp-content/uploads/2020/03/Powered-by-SA-5G-MEC-Based-Cloud-Game-Innovation-Practice-.pdf) (2020)

32. Han, J., Smith, B.: Cu-seeme vr immersive desktop teleconferencing. In: Proc. ACM Multimedia, pp. 199–207 (1997)

33. Nikolaevskiy, I.: Refactor framebuffer to store decoded frames history separately (i82be0eb3).gerrit code review. https://webrtc-review.googlesource.com/c/src/+/116686 (2019)

34. Winstein, K., Balakrishnan, H.: Mosh: An interactive remote shell for mobile clients. In Proc, USENIX ATC (2012)

35. Cloud gaming (beta) with xbox game pass | xbox. https://www.xbox.com/en-US/xbox-game-pass/cloud-gaming (2020)

36. Your games. your devices. play anywhere | nvidia geforce now. https://www.nvidia.com/en-us/geforce-now/ (2020)

37. Youtube vr - home - youtube vr. https://vr.youtube.com/ (2021)

38. Vr-interactive- we are interactive. https://vr-interactive.at/ (2021)

39. Facebook 360 video. https://facebook360.fb.com/ (2021)

40. Huawei video conferencing platform – huawei enterprise. https://e.huawei.com/en/solutions/enterprise-collaboration/videoconferencing-platform (2021)

41. Meeting and phone statistics –zoom help center. https://support.zoom.us/hc/en-us/articles/202920719-Meeting-and-phone-statistics (2021)

42. James Stringer. Pushing it to the limit – parsec at 240 frames per second with approximately 4-8 milliseconds of ... | parsec. https://parsec.app/blog/parsec-game-streaming-total-latency-at-240-frames-per-second-c0818cc0daa5 (2022)

43. Google meet and default video resolution - google meet community. https://support.google.com/meet/thread/58039897/google-meet-and-default-video-resolution (2021)

44. Adrian Pennington. So you say you're planning a 16k live stream... - nab amplify. https://amplify.nabshow.com/articles/so-you-say-youre-planning-a-16k-live-stream/ (2022)

45. Bulman, J., Garraghan, P.: A cloud gaming framework for dynamic graphical rendering towards achieving distributed game engines. In Proc, USENIX HotCloud (2020)

46. Tan, Z., Li, Y., Li, Q., Zhang, Z., Li, Z., Songwu, L.: Supporting mobile vr in lte networks: How close are we? Proc, ACM SIGMETRICS (2018)

47. Arun, V., Balakrishnan, H.: Copa: Practical delay-based congestion control for the internet. In Proc, USENIX NSDI (2018)

48. Carlucci, G., De Cicco, L., Holmer, S., Mascolo, S.: Congestion control for web real-time communication. IEEE/ACM Trans. Netw. (2017)

49. Carrascosa, M., Bellalta, B.: Cloud-gaming: Analysis of google stadia traffic. Comput. Commun. **188**, 99–116 (2022)

50. Mossad, O., Diab, K., Amer, I., Hefeeda, M.: Deepgame: Efficient video encoding for cloud gaming. In Proc, ACM Multimedia (2021)

51. Schwarz, H., Marpe, D., Wiegand, T.: Overview of the scalable video coding extension of the h. 264/avc standard. IEEE Trans. circ. syst. video technol. (2007)

52. Meng, Z., Guo, Y., Sun, C., Wang, B., Sherry, J., Liu, H. H., Xu, M.: Achieving Consistent low latency for wireless real time communications with the shortest control loop. In: Proc. ACM SIGCOMM (2022)

53. Dobrian, F., Sekar, V., Awan, A., Stoica, I., Joseph, D., Ganjam, A., Zhan, J., Zhang, H.: Understanding the impact of video quality on user engagement. In Proc, ACM SIGCOMM (2011)
54. Sabet, S. S., Schmidt, S., Zadtootaghaj, S., Naderi, B., Griwodz, C., Möller, S.: A latency compensation technique based on game characteristics to mitigate the influence of delay on cloud gaming quality of experience. In: Proc. ACM MMSys, pp. 15–25 (2020)
55. Processor benchmarks - geekbench browser. https://browser.geekbench.com/processor-benchmarks/, 2022
56. Gfxbench - unified graphics benchmark based on dxbenchmark (directx) and glbenchmark (opengl es). https://gfxbench.com/result.jsp, 2022
57. Prakash, A., Amrouch, H., Shafique, M., Mitra, T., Henkel, J.: Improving mobile gaming performance through cooperative cpu-gpu thermal management. In: Proc. ACM/EDAC/IEEE Design Automation Conference (DAC), pp. 1–6 (2016)
58. Lee, Y.G., Song, B.C.: An intra-frame rate control algorithm for ultralow delay h. 264/advanced video coding (avc). IEEE Trans. Circ. Syst. Video Technol., pp. 747–752 (2009)
59. Gallager, Robert G., Bertsekas, Dimitri P.: Section 3.3: The m/m/1 queuing system. In: Data networks (2nd Edition) (1992)
60. Trtx 2080 ti vs rtx 3080 ti game performance benchmarks (i7-8700k vs core i9-10900k) - gpucheck united states / usa. https://www.gpucheck.com/compare/nvidia-geforce-rtx-2080-ti-vs-nvidia-geforce-rtx-3080-ti/, 2021
61. Zhang, W., Qian, F., Han, B., Hui, P.: Deepvista: 16k panoramic cinema on your mobile device. In: Proceedings of the web conference, pp. 2232–2244 (2021)
62. Lin, C.C., Guo, J.I., Chang, H.C., Yang, Y.C., Chen, J.W., Tsai, M.C., Wang, J.S.: A 160kgate 4.5 kb skram h. 264 video decoder for hdtv applications. In: Proc. IEEE ISSCC, pp. 1596–1605 (2006)
63. Chuang, T.D., Tsung, P.K., Lin, P.C., Chang, L.M., Ma, T.C., Chen, Y.H., Chen, L.G.: A 59.5 mw scalable/multi-view video decoder chip for quad/3d full hdtv and video streaming applications. In: Proc. IEEE ISSCC, pp. 330–331 (2010)
64. Zhou, D., Zhou, J., He, X., Zhu, J., Kong, J., Liu, P., Goto, S.: A 530 mpixels/s 4096x2160@ 60fps h. 264/avc high profile video decoder chip. IEEE J. Solid-State Circ. **46**(4), 777–788 (2011)
65. Zhou, D., Zhou, J., Zhu, J., Liu, P., Goto, S.: A 2gpixel/s h. 264/avc hp/mvc video decoder chip for super hi-vision and 3dtv/ftv applications. In: Proc. IEEE International Solid-State Circuits Conference, pp. 224–226 (2012)
66. Zhou, D., Wang, S., Sun, H., Zhou, J., Zhu, J., Zhao, Y., Zhou, J., Zhang, S., Kimura, S., Yoshimura, T., et al.: An 8k h. 265/hevc video decoder chip with a new system pipeline design. IEEE J. Solid-State Cir. **52**(1), 113–126 (2017)
67. Lottarini, A., Ramirez, A., Coburn, J., Kim, Martha A., Ranganathan, P., Stodolsky, D., Wachsler, M.: vbench: Benchmarking video transcoding in the cloud. In: Proc. ASPLOS pp. 797–809 (2018)
68. Bruce, J., Mrak, M., Weerakkody, R.: Testing av1 and vvc - bbc r&d. https://www.bbc.co.uk/rd/blog/2019-05-av1-codec-streaming-processing-hevc-vvc (2019)
69. Azad, S., Song, W., Tjondronegoro, D.: Bitrate modeling of scalable videos using quantization parameter, frame rate and spatial resolution. In: Proc. IEEE ICASSP pp. 2334–2337 (2010)
70. multithreading - pin processor cpu isolation on windows - stack overflow. https://stackoverflow.com/questions/15324586/pin-processor-cpu-isolation-on-windows (2022)
71. Goyal, P., Agarwal, A., Netravali, R., Alizadeh, M., Balakrishnan, H.: Abc: A simple explicit congestion controller for wireless networks. In Proc, USENIX NSDI (2020)
72. Li, Y., Miao, R., Liu, H. H., Zhuang, Y., Feng, F., Tang, L., Cao, Z., Zhang, M., Kelly, F., Alizadeh, M., et al.: Hpcc: high precision congestion control. In: Proc. ACM SIGCOMM (2019)
73. Kingman, J.F.C., Atiyah, M.F.: The single server queue in heavy traffic. Oper. Manage., Critical Perspect. Bus. Manage (2003)
74. Jacobson, V.: Congestion avoidance and control. In Proc, ACM SIGCOMM (1988)

75. Pukelsheim, F.: The three sigma rule. The American Statistician (1994)
76. Sargent, M., Chu, J., Paxson, V., Allman, M.: Computing TCP's Retransmission Timer. IETF RFC 6298
77. Bridge, K., Satran, M.: Multitasking - win32 apps | microsoft docs. https://docs.microsoft.com/en-us/windows/win32/procthread/multitasking (2018)

Chapter 6
Transport Layer on Data Path: Differentiating Retransmissions

Abstract This chapter delves into how to optimize the transport layer for interactive multimedia streaming, focusing on differentiating retransmissions to enhance real-time performance. We explore both congestion control and packet loss recovery mechanisms and emphasize recent academic and industry proposals. A key highlight is Hairpin, a novel approach that co-designs redundancy and retransmission strategies to achieve lower latency and higher reliability for interactive streaming applications.

Keywords Interactive multimedia streaming · Packet loss recovery · Forward error correction · Transport layer latency

1 Transport Layer on Data Path

The transport layer is a highly focused component in Internet optimization, especially in the networking community represented by SIGCOMM/NSDI. The main function of the transport layer is to ensure that the data delivered by the application layer can reliably reach the receiving end in a timely manner. This is particularly challenging when latency varies, available bandwidth fluctuates, and network packet loss conditions change constantly. Therefore, the two main functions of the transport layer are rate control and reliable transmission. Rate control mainly focuses on congestion control on the Internet, while reliable transmission mainly focuses on packet loss recovery. Rate control works more on a relatively long timescale, trying to avoid long queues on the Internet and ensure its efficiency by adjusting congestion windows and rates. Reliable transmission, on the other hand, works more on a fine granularity, aiming to deliver one or a few lost packets to the receiving end. Below, we will briefly introduce the related work in these two aspects that are close to the goal of interactive multimedia streaming (Table 1).

© The Author(s), under exclusive license to Springer Nature Singapore Pte Ltd. 2024   87
Z. Meng and M. Xu, *Latency Optimization in Interactive Multimedia Streaming*,
SpringerBriefs in Computer Science, https://doi.org/10.1007/978-981-97-6729-8_6

Table 1 Related work on real-time multimedia optimization in the transport layer

Academic/industry proposals	Solutions	Main ideas
Sprout (NSDI'13) [1] GCC (MMSys'16) [2] NADA (RFC8698) [3] Scream (RFC8298) [4] Copa (NSDI'18) [5] Vivace (NSDI'18) [6]	Congestion Control	By adapting the sending rate to bandwidth to reduce latency
WebRTC (ICIP'13) [7] AdaptFEC (MM'19) [8] Tambur (NSDI'23) [9] TLP (RFC8985) [10] Hairpin (NSDI'24) [11]	Packet Loss Recovery	By reducing retransmissions to reduce end-to-end latency

1.1 Congestion Control

Congestion control has a history of more than 40 years—we recommend the readers to read the book *TCP Congestion Control: A Systems Approach*[1] for a deeper understanding. Among them, low-latency congestion control has long been a concern for network researchers. Early congestion control algorithms such as Reno [12] and Cubic [13] aimed to improve network resource utilization by occupying queues as much as possible, but this led to an increase in end-to-end latency. In recent years, a more widely used algorithm is BBR, proposed by Google in 2016 [14]. BBR estimates the bottleneck bandwidth and round-trip time of the link to determine how many data packets should be in the network and sends data packets at this rate. In this way, BBR no longer needs to occupy the bottleneck queue and can achieve lower latency. In addition, there are algorithms such as Sprout [1], Verus [15], and Copa [5] that further use latency information to perform more accurate rate control for the TCP protocol. For example, Verus [15] is a congestion control algorithm that specifically adapts to the channel fluctuations of cellular networks by adapting latency estimation; Copa [5] adjusts the congestion window on the endpoint by using the signal of latency fluctuations. They can both effectively achieve lower latency.

In the field of multimedia streaming, these algorithms have also been deployed to some extent. For example, Facebook has tested the Copa algorithm in its live streaming business [16] and achieved good results. In addition, there are many congestion control algorithms specifically designed for interactive multimedia streaming applications. For example, Google proposed the GCC [2] algorithm, which is used in the WebRTC framework. The GCC algorithm controls the sending rate by using delay gradient information—measuring the delay of each packet is usually inaccurate because distinguishing between queue delay and transmission delay has always been a problem for end-to-end congestion control algorithms. Therefore, the GCC algorithm focuses on the difference in delay between two packets—called the delay

---

[1] https://tcpcc.systemsapproach.org/.

gradient—for rate control: when the packet delay is gradually increasing, the bottle-neck queue in the network is probably accumulating. At this time, GCC will reduce its sending rate and vice versa. In addition, Cisco and Ericsson have also proposed NADA [3] and SCREAM [4] algorithms, respectively, to specifically optimize real-time audio and video transmission. They further use some information, including Explicit Congestion Notification (ECN), to reduce end-to-end transmission latency.

However, as we introduced in Chap. 1, even though congestion control has made many efforts to control latency jitter, existing algorithms still struggle to achieve satisfactory latency for interactive multimedia streaming applications. Users still suffer from poor network experiences in many situations. On the one hand, this is certainly because applications have increasingly higher demands for latency and smoothness, and on the other hand, it also shows the limitations of purely end-to-end congestion control algorithm optimization. This work aims to explore the new performance bottlenecks in the transport layer and congestion control based on existing work.

1.2 Packet Loss Recovery

Packet loss recovery is an important issue in the transport layer, and its purpose is to ensure the reliability of transmission when packet loss occurs in the network. A significant feature that distinguishes the TCP protocol from the UDP protocol is its ability to recover lost packets in the kernel effectively. For most applications, including interactive multimedia streaming, the main recovery method when packet loss occurs in the network is retransmitting the lost packet. Retransmitting packets also requires many design considerations, mainly on how to determine if a packet is lost rather than out of order or delayed. Initially, TCP used Retransmission Time-out (RTO) to make this judgment—if the original packet's acknowledgment is not received after waiting for a period of time (usually 1 s or 200 milliseconds), the sender will choose to retransmit the packet [17]. Subsequently, the Fast Retransmit mechanism allowed three consecutive identical acknowledgments to trigger retrans-mission quickly. Recent work has proposed Tail Loss Probe (TLP) [10] and other mechanisms that can still promptly retransmit discarded packets when waiting for three identical acknowledgments takes too long.

Another line of research is to introduce redundancy for packet loss recovery. This approach is also easy to understand: for example, when the sender intends to send three data packets, the sender can encode a fourth packet using Forward Error Correction (FEC) and send all four packets together in case any packets may be lost. As long as the receiver receives any three packets, it can recover the fourth packet. In this direction, one approach is to use existing FEC technology but dynamically adjust its parameters according to the current network state: when the network packet loss rate is high, the proportion of redundant packets is higher. For example, Bolot [18] and USF [19] algorithms adjust parameters based on the historical packet loss recovery situation and their recovery capabilities. In this direction, there are also algorithms for

WebRTC's FEC parameters [20], where some of the recent algorithms even use deep reinforcement learning and other machine learning tools to predict network status further and optimize redundancy parameters [21]. They all achieve good performance in different environments, effectively recovering lost packets.

In addition to optimizing redundancy parameters, another category of work is to design redundancy coding mechanisms directly. This usually requires a strong knowledge of groups, rings, fields, and other mathematical concepts. Many of these works have also been published in information theory journals, such as *IEEE Transactions on Information Theory*. Representative works include AdaptFEC [8], and other coding mechanisms by [22, 23]. However, these algorithms are difficult to deploy in practice due to their high complexity. In fact, XOR codes are currently the most widely used redundancy coding mechanisms in interactive multimedia streaming. Even slightly more complex codes like Reed-Solomon (RS) codes are not yet mature.

In this chapter, we will introduce a piece of work that jointly optimizes the two types of work, redundancy and retransmission. From a practical perspective, this work does not propose a new redundancy coding mechanism but tries to optimize existing coding mechanisms. Another highlight of this work is to optimize the packet loss recovery mechanism from the perspective of latency fluctuations.

2   Introduction

A major challenge to control the deadline misses comes from the high instantaneous loss rate on the Internet. Due to the spatial dependency within video frames and temporal dependency between video frames, interactive streaming expects packets to be reliably delivered [24]. However, from our measurement of our edge-based cloud gaming service in production with O(10,000) users, sessions can experience a drastically high *instantaneous* loss rate. Although the average loss rate is considerably low by mechanisms such as proper rate control, our measurement observes that more than 2% of video frames suffer from an instantaneous loss rate of 20% or higher (§3.1). It indicates that those lost packets are concentrated on a few frames. Thus, although the network RTT can be very low with edge deployments, retransmissions of lost packets take additional time and will consequently violate the deadline. Thus, optimizing the loss recovery mechanisms to control the deadline miss rate (DMR) of video frames is essential.

Unfortunately, existing solutions to recover packet losses cannot meet the stringent DMR requirements with a reasonable bandwidth cost. As shown in Fig. 1, one line of research efforts (the vertical dimension) is devoted to quickly retransmitting lost packets, such as probe timeout (PTO) [10], from the transport layer. However, merely retransmitting lost packets cannot meet the requirement of interactive streaming—the DMR is much higher than 0.1%. Another line of effort (the horizontal dimension) is devoted to adaptive forward error correction (FEC) so that the client might be able to recover packets based on redundant packets without retransmission [20].

Yet, redundancy-based solutions come with a considerable bandwidth cost of 20% or more due to the high instantaneous loss rate. For content providers, such a high bandwidth cost will drastically increase operating expenses and degrade users' video quality. To the best of our knowledge, none of the existing solutions *jointly optimized* retransmission and redundancy. Even when adopted together, such an orthogonal design of redundancy and retransmission still cannot meet the bandwidth cost and DMR needs for interactive streaming.

Our key insight is to break the trade-off by differentiating retransmission packets. Edge-based interactive streaming services can achieve an average RTT of 10–20ms between application servers and users by deploying the servers on the edge [25–27]. In this case, limited times of retransmissions (but not too many) are tolerable for applications that have a deadline of 50–200ms (§3.1). However, the strategy for retransmission packets must be different from the initial transmission packets. The volume of retransmission packets is much less than initial transmission packets since packet loss is always the minority. Yet, retransmission packets have a much tighter time requirement since they have already consumed time. This brings new changes to reduce the bandwidth cost and the DMR at the same time (§3.4). By differentiating the strategies for initial transmission and retransmission packets, we can break the trade-off between bandwidth cost and DMR.

Differentiating retransmissions for a different redundancy rate is the main insight for this work, which will help a lot with the performance. We then introduce Hairpin,[2] a new packet loss recovery mechanism to jointly optimize packet retransmission and redundancy for edge-based interactive streaming (§4.3). However, as later elaborated in §4.2, to further analytically optimize the performance, we still face the challenge of (1) the dependency of decisions and future states, (2) the multi-dimensionality of decisions, and (3) the convoluted goal of DMR and bandwidth cost. In response, Hairpin further formulates the problem into a Markov decision process (MDP), which is known for efficiently optimizing the temporal dependency [29]. We then

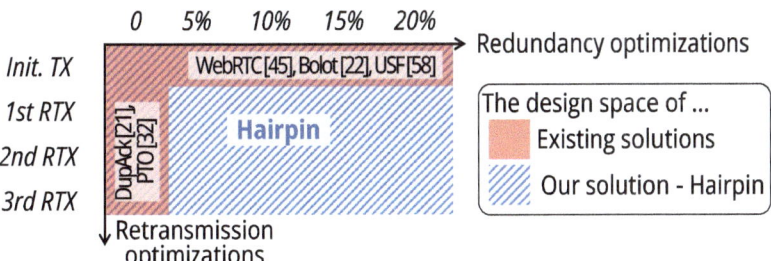

Fig. 1 An illustration of the design space of existing solutions and Hairpin. By co-designing the redundancy and retransmission at the transport layer, Hairpin is able to break the existing trade-off between bandwidth cost and deadline miss rate

---

[2] In badminton, a hairpin shot is played when the shuttle is very near to the ground, and the net (the deadline of a shot) [28].

encode the decisions and states into nodes of MDP to reduce the complexity and achieve the optimal result.

3 Background and Motivations

We introduce the interactive streaming (§3.1), present our measurement of packet losses (§3.2), analyze why existing solutions are insufficient (§3.3), and motivate the design of Hairpin (§3.4).

3.1 Interactive Multimedia Streaming

Besides the stringent deadline requirement required by interactive multimedia streaming applications, there are two additional features:

Reliable delivery Interactive streaming also requires reliable delivery for each frame. For commercial video codecs, failing to deliver a part of the frame will lead to severe image quality degradation. Moreover, the loss of one frame would also lead to blurring for the subsequent frames due to the dependency between frames.[3]

Therefore, existing interactive streaming services usually try their best to reliably deliver frames. For example, industrial frameworks (e.g., WebRTC) [7, 20] and academic efforts [18, 19, 22] propose to employ forward error correction (FEC) to recover lost packets at the receiver if possible, and will retransmit lost packets if the recovery fails [31].

Low bandwidth cost The bandwidth cost is still one of the largest operating expenses in our and other cloud gaming services [32]. Moreover, to achieve a satisfactory user experience, interactive streaming must stream with high video resolution and frame rate (e.g., 60 fps and >1080p for cloud gaming), which requires high goodput to support. Given the low operating expenses and high video quality requirements for users, we need to control the bandwidth cost in packet loss recovery.

3.2 Packet Losses in Edge-Based Interactive Streaming

Our observation from our cloud gaming service is that although the median loss rate is as low as 10^{-3}, the *instantaneous* loss rate could be very high. In our measurement campaign as described in §3.1, we also calculate the *session-level loss rate*, which is the ratio of total lost packets in one user session (minutes to hours, containing at least

---

[3] Mechanisms such as scalable video coding (SVC) allow limited packet losses yet reduce the bandwidth efficiency and require client support [30].

Fig. 2 Distribution of
session-level and frame-level
packet loss rates

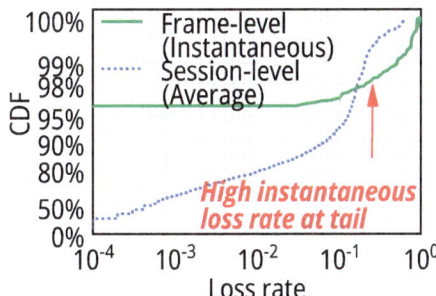

O(10,000) frames), to reflect the average loss rate over a long timescale. We then calculate *frame-level loss rate*, which is the ratio of lost packets within one frame (tens of milliseconds), to show the instantaneous loss rate over a short timescale. For example, if a session has 1M packets and 10 lost, the session-level average loss rate is 0.01%. Meanwhile, if these 10 packets belong to the same video frame, which has 50 packets in total, the frame-level instantaneous loss rate will be 20% for that frame and 0% for other frames.

As shown in Fig. 2, the session-level loss rate is 0.05% at the median, which is comparable to similar measurements [33]. However, the instantaneous frame-level loss rate could be very high: 2% frames lose more than 20% of their packets within one frame. Such a high instantaneous packet loss poses a great challenge in controlling the deadline miss rate to 10^{-3} or lower—we can no longer ignore these transient behaviors and have to deliver video frames in time even when the instantaneous loss rate is high.

Moreover, reducing the sending rate cannot easily mitigate these packet losses. To achieve low latency, most CCAs in interactive streaming use *delay* as the signal to reduce the sending rate (e.g., BBR [14], Copa [5], GCC [2]). In this case, congestion losses rarely happen since the sending rate has already been reduced based on an increasing delay in advance, which has also been measured in related work [2]. Our online measurements unveil similar observations: our cloud gaming service has already adopted a delay-based CCA similar to GCC [2], which is widely deployed in interactive streaming applications such as Chrome and Stadia. We further demonstrate the weak correlation between RTT[4] increases and packet losses in our measurement in §3.4. As shown in Fig. 2, losses are still outstanding at the tail, indicating that merely controlling the bit rate or frame rate is insufficient to avoid edge-based interactive streaming packet losses.

---

[4] In this chapter, we use RTT to represent the delay at the network layer that does not contain the time of retransmission. We use application delay to refer to the delay at the application layer that contains the retransmissions.

3.3   Why Existing Solutions Fail?

As we discussed in §2, packet losses contribute a lot to deadline misses. Thus, we investigate why existing packet loss recovery mechanisms are insufficient for edge-based interactive streaming. Existing solutions mainly fall into two categories as follows:

Retransmissions Existing transport protocols (e.g., TCP) rely on retransmissions to cope with packet losses. Merely relying on retransmissions is insufficient to achieve an extremely low DMR for interactive streaming frames at the magnitude of 0.1% or lower. For example, when the packet loss rate is instantaneously 20%, there would still be 0.16% packets lost even after 3 retransmissions. Note that since there could be tens to hundreds of packets per frame, being unable to deliver even one packet would violate the deadline requirement of that frame since interactive streaming requires all packets to be reliably delivered (§3.1). Thus, the DMR of frames is still considerably high when relying on retransmissions and rate controls only.

Redundancy-based algorithms There are also several solutions in interactive streaming with redundancy mechanisms, such as FEC. However, existing adaptive FEC solutions from both the industry [7, 20] and academia [18, 19, 22] optimize the FEC parameters only for the initial transmission. They adjust the number of FEC packets according to the loss rate and retransmit packets as usual when packet loss occurs. Note that packet losses are not deterministic: when the transient loss probability increases to 20%, it does not mean precisely one packet loss every five packets. In this case, to achieve an extremely low DMR of 10^{-3} or lower, FEC rates need to be much higher than the loss rate, leading to severe bandwidth costs. For example, WebRTC, a state-of-the-art interactive streaming framework, will send 100% redundant packets during this short timescale of high instantaneous loss rate for initial transmissions. In this case, there will be considerable bandwidth costs, and the DMR might still not be satisfied.

3.4   Motivations

Therefore, with the reduced RTT, retransmissions are tolerable to some extent for edge-based interactive streaming. In this case, we have the following observations on how and what to retransmit.

RTT being much lower than the deadline enables the joint optimization of redundancy and retransmission As we discussed before, with an RTT of 10–20 ms and a deadline of 50–150 ms, multiple retransmissions are tolerable to some extent. This enables the joint optimization of redundancy and retransmission, which results in benefits in two folds:

- Reduce the deadline miss rate. In existing FEC mechanisms, many of the deadline misses come from the packet losses in the retransmissions. When adding redundancy packets over retransmission packets, we could effectively avoid the loss of retransmission packets and further reduce the deadline miss rate.

- Save bandwidth costs. To achieve the same DMR, the bandwidth cost of adding redundancy to retransmissions is significantly lower than that of only adding redundancy to initial transmissions. This is because retransmission packets are always the minority in bandwidth consumption—duplicating retransmissions will only introduce a little bandwidth cost, but could have significant DMR improvements.

When more rounds of retransmissions are tolerated (e.g., with smaller RTTs), the joint optimization will have more significant benefits. We are thus motivated to utilize the retransmission chances enabled by edge deployments and jointly optimize the redundancy and retransmission mechanisms.

Loss recovery adaptions at the server are possible Dynamically optimizing tail cases with high instantaneous loss rates needs quick adaptation. According to our measurement, the feedback loop between the server and client is smaller than the duration of loss events, making the joint optimization of redundancy and retransmission practical. This comes in two folds:

- The feedback loop does not inflate with the increase in the loss rate. We measure the RTT of our cloud gaming service and categorize them into different frame loss rate intervals. As shown in Fig. 3a, the distribution of RTT does not significantly vary with the frame loss rate. The RTT in WiFi increases with the increase of frame loss rate (e.g., due to retransmissions at the link layer [34]). Nevertheless, even when the frame-level loss rate is 30% (the dashed green curve in Fig. 3b), 60% of those acknowledged packets have an RTT of less than 25ms. This indicates (i) the server is able to detect the network condition changes quickly, and (ii) there are still multiple transmission chances when the instantaneous loss rate increases.
- The duration of loss events is transient but still longer than several feedback loops. We measure the duration of lossy frames in our cloud gaming service and present the results in Fig. 4. According to our measurements, most loss events span multiple RTTs. For example, 70% of frames with a frame-level loss rate of >10% will last more than 2 frames in Ethernet sessions, which is several times the median RTT

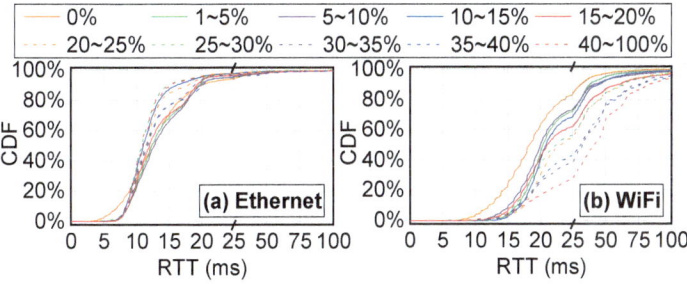

Fig. 3 RTT distributions measured in production, categorized by the frame-level loss rate. Note that retransmissions are not counted

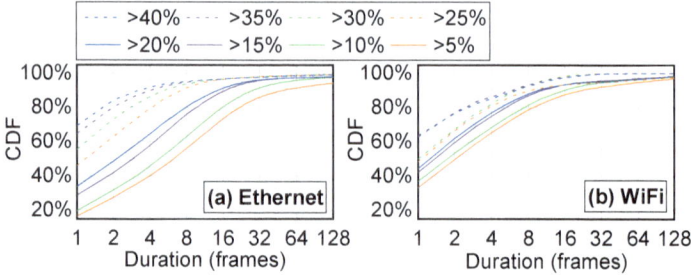

Fig. 4 The distribution of the duration of each loss event measured in production. We measure the duration of each time when the loss rate is larger than different thresholds (5%, ..., 40%). Loss rates are measured at the frame level. The network type is reported from our cloud gaming clients. Better viewed in color

(12ms) at the frame rate of 60fps. Therefore, the reaction from the server is still effective in alleviating packet losses by adjusting the redundancy parameters.

4 Hairpin Optimizer

As we discussed above, edge-based interactive streaming needs to reduce the deadline miss rate and bandwidth cost. For clarity, we first present the formula of frame deadline miss rate (DMR) and bandwidth cost (BWC):

$$
\begin{aligned}
\text{DMR} &= \frac{\#\text{Frames arrive after the deadline}}{\#\text{Total frames}} \\
\text{BWC} &= \frac{\text{Redundancy}_{\text{byte}} + \text{Retransmission}_{\text{byte}}}{\text{Data}_{\text{byte}}}
\end{aligned}
\tag{1}
$$

A higher DMR or BWC means more frequent stutters or higher operating expenses respectively, both of which interactive streaming service providers will try to avoid. Note that pushing DMR to an extremely low level is critical since the lower it is, the better user's experience is going to be.

In this section, we first summarize some intuitions in the design space of joint optimization of redundancy rate and retransmission and present a strawman solution (§4.1). We then present the design challenges in the joint optimization of retransmission and redundancy (§4.2). We address these challenges by providing a Markov chain-based optimization algorithm to efficiently improve both the DMR and BWC (§4.3). We finally discuss how Hairpin handles the inaccuracy in measurement, the overhead in online deployment, and other practical issues in §4.4.

4.1 Basic Idea and Strawman Solution

Differentiating retransmissions from initial transmissions The most important insight in this chapter is to understand the significance of differentiating retransmissions from initial transmissions. In other words, we want an adaptive redundancy rate based on the planning of multiple transmission chances. The short RTT of edge-based interactive streaming enables packets to have more than one transmission chance without violating the deadline. The ratio of RTT and remaining time t indicates the potential number of (re)transmissions. For example, when the current RTT is 20ms and packets still have 40ms toward their deadline, the ratio follows $\frac{t}{\text{RTT}} = \frac{40\text{ms}}{20\text{ms}} = 2$, indicating that these packets could be approximately transmitted twice before the deadline. Packets with more transmission chances could better utilize the potential retransmissions to deliver packets before the deadline, which has already been discussed in §3.4. Therefore, our basic idea is to take future transmission chances into consideration when optimizing the redundancy rate. When one batch of packets has more foreseeable transmission chances (i.e., the deadline is still far away), we could reduce the redundancy rate to save bandwidth costs. When the remaining time for these packets gets closer to the deadline due to retransmissions, we could further increase the redundancy rate to avoid deadline misses.

Strawman solution: RTT-aware adaptive FEC algorithm Therefore, a strawman solution is to (i) add redundancy to both initial transmissions and retransmissions and (ii) consider the remaining transmission chance in the optimization of the redundancy rate. Since there have already been existing solutions on the redundancy rate based on network conditions [18–20], we could introduce a multiplier controlled by the transmission chance over the existing redundancy rate optimizations, i.e., a strawman solution is to reduce the redundancy rate when there are many transmission chances, and increase it when transmission chances are few. Thus, we could enhance these algorithms by introducing a factor over the results from existing algorithms.

FEC consists of two parameters (d, k), where d data packets and k redundant packets are sent as a *block*. The block is composed for the convenience of FEC encoding. If there are up to k packets lost in an FEC block (d, k), an ideal FEC decoder can recover all data packets with any remaining packets [35–37]. We denote $\beta = \frac{k}{d}$ as the FEC redundancy rate, and d as the FEC block size.

Specifically, given a packet loss rate α and bitrate B, assume one of the state-of-the-art solutions has already determined that $\beta_0(\alpha, B)$ should be the optimized redundancy. We could then increase or decrease the redundancy rate $\beta_0(\alpha, B)$ based on the remaining transmission chance $\frac{t}{\text{RTT}}$, i.e.:

$$\beta(\alpha, B, \text{RTT}, t) = k \cdot \frac{\text{RTT}}{t} \cdot \beta_0(\alpha, B) \tag{2}$$

where k is a coefficient to adjust how aggressive the strawman solution is going to increase or decrease the redundancy rate.

In fact, such a strawman solution is enough to push the Pareto frontier of DMR-BWC forward. However, it confronts a series of shortcomings, which prevents the operator from further improvements in performance. We will elaborate on these challenges in the following section.

4.2   Design Challenges

Although we have presented a heuristic RTT-aware adaptive FEC algorithm as above, it is still challenging to optimize these parameters due to the following reasons.

Temporal dependency: cascading decision-making between transmission rounds
When considering multiple transmission chances, the decision of FEC parameters of one round of transmission would cascadingly affect the optimization of the next round. For example, if we aggressively add a high redundancy rate to a group of packets, the number of packet losses will then be decreased. On the contrary, a low redundancy rate for the same group of packets would probabilistically increase the number of packet losses under the same network condition. However, these packet losses bring more packets to retransmit in the next round. If we consider all actions for F packets for the foreseeable L rounds of transmission, the action space will be extremely large: Since for each redundancy decision, there are F possible scenarios of the number of packets to transmit in the next round (depending on how many packets are lost), the number of variables that we need to optimize will be $O(F^L)$.[5] Therefore, in the enlarged action space over multiple retransmissions, it is challenging to optimize efficiently. Moreover, the conditional probability between scenarios is not linear (e.g., hypergeometric for individually independently and identically distributed losses). Therefore, using traditional optimization methods such as integer programming in an extremely large action space is impractical. We need to coordinate the choices in different rounds of transmission to achieve optimal performance.

Spatial dependency: redundancy rate and block size are tightly coupled Even in a single round, different variables (e.g., redundancy rate, block size, etc.) still have complicated dependencies on each other. This goes to the following aspects:

(a) Number of packets to transmit in one round affects redundancy rates The number of packets to transmit in the different rounds varies, depending on how many data packets are lost during the last transmission. The penalty of redundancy rate on BWC also varies according to the number of packets to retransmit. For example, when there are few packets to retransmit, even adding a redundancy rate of 100% for retransmissions would not consume too much bandwidth, as also discussed in §3.4. Therefore, fewer data packets to retransmit would encourage a more aggressive redundancy rate. The strawman solution is not aware of the dependency here, leading to its suboptimal result.

---

[5] For a frame with 50 packets (F=50), and 5 potential transmission rounds (L=5, e.g., RTT is 20ms and deadline is 100ms), this turns into 10^8 variables.

(b) Dispersion of blocks might lead to deadline misses when using larger blocks Due to the bandwidth limit at the bottleneck link, packets sent out at the same time could be dispersed [38] and arrive at the receiver one by one. In this case, constructing large blocks will increase the delay in waiting for all packets at the receiver. Since packet losses can only be determined after the completion of one block, smaller blocks may know earlier whether they need retransmission and enjoy additional transmission chances before the deadline. For example, in Fig. 5, due to the early determination of packet loss, the retransmission of data packets for small blocks could arrive at the receiver before the deadline, while no packets could arrive before the deadline for large blocks. We quantify the influence of block size by measuring the receiving time of FEC blocks from our service online with different block sizes. As we can see in Fig. 6a and b, with a block size of 50 packets, more than 10% blocks could span 10ms at the receiver, which is even comparable to the RTT. Also smaller block sizes might also be beneficial when the loss rate is higher than the redundancy rate. As illustrated in Fig. 5, when the first four packets are lost during the transmission, data packet #3 could still be successfully delivered for a small block size (the case above in Fig. 5). For large blocks, there is no way to recover any lost packet if the loss rate is larger than the redundancy rate.

Convoluted goal: deadline miss rate and bandwidth cost Unlike latency or throughput, which we can directly measure, estimating the expected deadline miss rate needs to consider multiple potential transmission rounds. In this way, the straw-

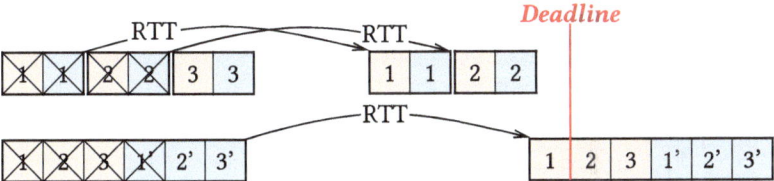

Fig. 5 Smaller block sizes in one frame could have better performance. Scenarios above and below represent using small and large blocks. Data and FEC packets are shaded orange and blue

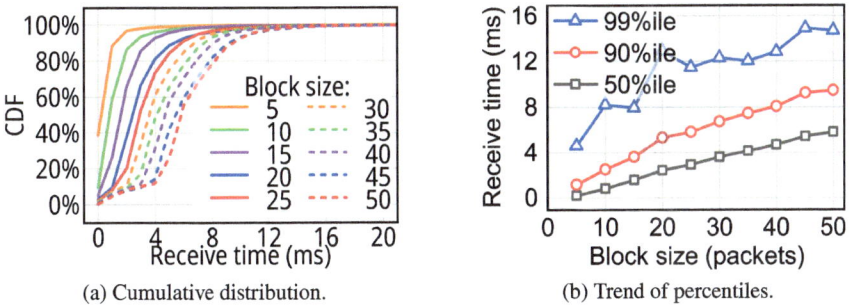

(a) Cumulative distribution.   (b) Trend of percentiles.

Fig. 6 Block receiving time with different block sizes. FEC blocks are burstily sent out at the server side. Figure 6b is processed from Fig. 6a. Better viewed in color

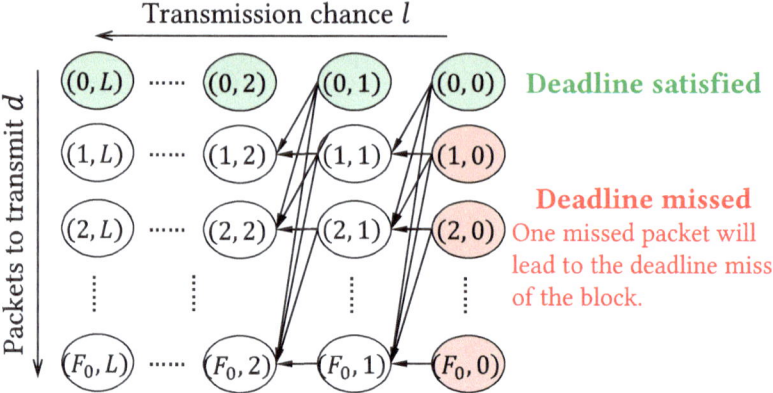

Fig. 7 The absorbing Markov chain in redundancy rate optimization at a given loss rate and frame size. l is the estimated remaining transmission chances for the packets to transmit

man solution, without explicitly estimating whether that frame is going to miss the deadline or not, will have suboptimal results. For example, the relationship between the packet loss rate and the success rate of delivering a video frame with tens of packets in a single round is *hypergeometric*, even under the identical and independent distribution (i.i.d.) assumption. Considering multiple future rounds together will only make the relationship between deadline miss rate and network conditions more convoluted. Moreover, some applications or even the same application in different operating regions may have different preferences over deadline miss rate v.s. bandwidth cost. The traffic cost in some regions might be higher than in others, and some applications may give it all for the user's experience while others may not. Therefore, we need to explicitly optimize toward the goal to achieve the optimal result.

4.3 Model Formulation and Optimization

We have the following designs to address the challenges above.

Encode the temporal dependency in multi-round planning into edges in Markov chain Markov chain is widely used in the optimization of the sequential decision-making process (e.g., reinforcement learning [29]). With the Markov chain, we can formulate the loss detection between two rounds of (re)transmission into the transition between two Markov nodes. In this case, by only focusing on the optimal parameters between the transition of the current state and its potential states in the next round, we could decouple the cascading effects of the transitions between neighbor nodes, which reduces the action space significantly.

Encoding the spatial dependency between variables into nodes in the Markov chain To ensure the number of packets to transmit is considered in the optimization, we build a 2-D Markov chain, with two dimensions as the transmission chance and the number of packets to transmit. We present the state transition of our Markov chain in Fig. 7. Each node is represented by (d, l), where d denotes the number of remaining data packets to transmit, and l represents the remaining transmission chance for those packets. Our goal is to find out the optimal redundancy rate for node (B, L), where B is a given block size, and L is the remaining transmission chance from Eq. (3). In this case, both the temporal dependency and spatial correlation between variables could be formulated into this 2-D Markov chain.

Explicitly optimize deadline miss rate and bandwidth cost with Markov chain formulation We finally provide an explicit expression of the deadline miss rate and bandwidth cost for multi-round optimization within the formulation of MDP. We inversely calculate the DMR and BWC at different states from the last chance to transmit (as the last layer of the Markov chain) to the first chance to transmit (as the first layer of the Markov chain). In this way, the transition probabilities between states could be directly iterated. We further decouple the optimization of redundancy rate and block size to improve the optimization efficiency.

We present the analytical model and the algorithm below. In interactive streaming, frames are continuously generated and sent out from the server. There are thousands to millions of frames within one stream, depending on the specific application, where the retransmission of previous frames overlaps with the transmission of subsequent frames. Therefore, similar to the finite element analysis in mechanics [39], we pick one frame from the stream and analyze the expected DMR and BWC of that frame. The expected DMR and BWC of one frame should be consistent with the DMR and BWC of a stream. We list all notations that are going to be used in Table 2. Specifically, Hairpin optimizes the FEC parameters as follows:

Step 1: Calculating remaining transmission chance Given the current network RTT, the remaining time toward deadline T, the bottleneck bandwidth Θ, and a certain block size d, the remaining transmission chance L could be calculated as:

$$L = \frac{T - d/\Theta}{\text{RTT}} \tag{3}$$

Step 2: Generating absorbing Markov chain We then calculate the optimal redundancy rate given the current loss rate α and frame size F. We iteratively calculate the

Table 2 Notations in §4

Notation	Explanation
Inputs	
α	Network loss rate
T	Remaining time till the deadline
RTT	The network round-trip time
Θ	The network bottleneck bandwidth
F	The frame size of that frame
Intermediate variables	
L	Remaining transmission chance
$l(n, r)$	The number of lost packets at the r-th layer with n data packets
$k(n, r)$	The number of redundant packets at the r-th layer with n data packets
DMR	Deadline miss rate
BWC	Bandwidth cost
Outputs	
β_i	Redundancy rate at the i-th layer
b_i	FEC block size at the i-th layer

absorbing Markov chain from layer $l - 1$ to layer l. For the node (d, l), at a certain redundancy rate β, its DMR follows:

$$\text{DMR}(d, l; \beta) = \sum_{d'=0}^{d} p\left((d, l) \rightarrow (d', l - 1); \beta\right) \cdot \text{DMR}(d', l - 1) \quad (4)$$

where $p((d, l) \rightarrow (d', l - 1); \beta)$ is the transition probability from (d, l) to $(d', l - 1)$ and could be calculated based on the current loss rate α and redundancy rate β. Similarly, the BWC could also be updated as:

$$\text{BWC}(d, l; \beta) = \beta \frac{d}{F} + \sum_{d'=0}^{d} p((d, l) \rightarrow (d', l - 1); \beta) \cdot \text{BWC}(d', l - 1) \quad (5)$$

where the latter term is the additional BWC introduced in this layer l. Then, we calculate the optimal β for (d, l):

$$\beta_{\text{opt}}(d, l) = \arg \min_{\beta} \text{utility}(\text{DMR}(d, l; \beta), \text{BWC}(d, l; \beta)) \quad (6)$$

and have $\text{DMR}(d, l) = \text{DMR}(d, l; \beta_{\text{opt}})$ and $BWC(d, l) = BWC(d, l; \beta_{\text{opt}})$. Here, utility$(\text{DMR}, \text{BWC})$ is the utility function that balances preferences for low DMR and low BWC. For simplicity, we adopt a linear combination of DMR and BWC as the optimization goal:

$$\text{utility}(\text{DMR}, \text{BWC}) = \text{DMR} + \lambda \cdot \text{BWC} \tag{7}$$

Note that Hairpin does not fall into the same trade-off between DMR and BWC as baselines but improves both DMR and BWC. In practice, service providers can adjust the coefficient λ to balance stuttering events and bandwidth costs in different scenarios. A lower λ indicates that users prefer the deadline miss rate more than bandwidth costs.

Therefore, the redundancy rate for (B, L) could be optimized accordingly. After calculating all nodes at the layer l, we could then calculate the DMR and BWC at the layer $l + 1$, until the node (B, L) has been calculated. Since the iterations between nodes are linear, as long as the utility function is monotonic to DMR and BWC (e.g., linear relationship), the optimality still holds.

We set $DMR(d, 0)$ to 1 for $d > 0$ since one missed packet would lead to the miss of the block (shaded green). We also set all $DMR(0, l)$ to 0 since there is no remaining packet to transmit. The BWC for all these boundary nodes is set to 0. Note that different block sizes and remaining transmission chance could multiplex the same chain to accelerate the optimization since the chain only depends on loss rate α and frame size F.

Step 3: Calculating optimal block size We enumerate the possible block sizes from 1 to the frame size, calculate the DMR and BWC for each block according to the chain in Step 2, and finally find the optimal block size in terms of a given utility function. Not surprisingly, when the bottleneck bandwidth is high (i.e., the dispersion is insignificant), the optimal block size for most scenarios is the frame size. Nevertheless, constructing smaller blocks could achieve better DMR when the dispersion is significant. Operators could optimize the block size for improvements at the last mile.

During the optimization of block sizes, we also optimize the trade-off of when a loss has been detected, whether to retransmit that packet as soon as possible or wait for other packets to formulate an FEC block. On recovery ability, constructing several lost packets into one FEC block might be more effective than individually retransmitting (or duplicating, if with redundancy) each packet. We calculate the failure rate of delivering these packets when there are different numbers of packets to retransmit at different redundancy rates and loss rates and present the results in Fig. 8.

When a few packets need retransmission, whether duplicating or constructing FEC blocks, there is no major difference (dashed line and solid lines shaded green). However, when optimizing at the *tail* for interactive streaming, there could be multiple packet losses within one frame. Therefore, considering each frame could contain tens of packets, it is possible to suffer losses of 4 packets or more at the tail. Constructing FEC blocks for these retransmission packets could reduce the failure rate of delivering packets by several magnitudes.

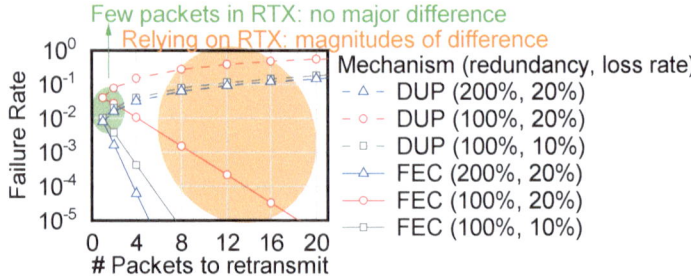

Fig. 8 A theoretical illustration of the failure rate of retransmitting different numbers of packets by per-packet duplication or constructing FEC blocks. The failure rate of DUP increases with the number of packets to retransmit since we need to ensure every data packet is delivered. We vary the redundancy rate and loss rate

Step 4: Getting the optimal parameters Finally, based on network conditions and remaining time toward a deadline, Hairpin can calculate the optimal block size based on Step 3, and the optimal redundancy rate with the block size based on Step 2.

4.4   Deployment Discussions

In §4, we analytically optimize the FEC parameters given certain network conditions. The reality might be more complicated than the theoretical model. In this section, we discuss several practical concerns of Hairpin.

Reducing computational overhead online Hairpin adopts an optimization-based algorithm, which might not scale to production-scale deployments in terms of computational overhead. Since the optimization needs to run frequently (approximately every frame) and scale to tens of thousands of users simultaneously, it should be computation-efficient and time-efficient. In response, we do an offline step of enumerating the state space and solving each specific instance. Then, in the online step, the algorithm will be reduced to a simple table lookup toward pre-computed optimized redundancy parameters. We enumerate the state space of Hairpin as below.

1. Remaining transmission chance: 1 to 10.
2. Loss rate: 0% to 50% with quantization of 1%.
3. Frame size: 5 to 60 packets with quantization of 5 packets.
4. Number of packets to (re)transmit: 5 to 60 packets with quantization of 5 packets.

Hairpin then stores the best redundancy rate and block size under different conditions.

Handling network fluctuations We discuss how Hairpin handles the fluctuations in network conditions. For RTT, as presented in Fig. 3, RTT does not increase too much—the median RTT always allows Hairpin to have 3–5 transmission chances no matter the loss rate. Moreover, we further measure the network conditions in

Hairpin with a short sliding window to make sure Hairpin has the most recent network conditions. In this case, the transient fluctuation of RTT could be reflected in the optimization results immediately.

Handling various loss patterns In this chapter, when given a certain loss rate, Hairpin assumes the pattern of packet losses is identically and independently distributed (in the transition probability of Eq. 4). Note that the duration of a certain loss rate still follows the results of the online measurement in Fig. 4. In practical deployment, working with FEC codecs that could recover from different loss patterns (bursty or arbitrary) [35], Hairpin could also handle different loss patterns since Hairpin only focuses on how many packets within a block are lost. Since our data is collected frame by frame, if the burstiness spans over several frames, it will be directly reflected in the value of loss rates. If the burstiness spans within the frame, no matter how the pattern changes, the number of lost packets will not change, which does not affect the recovery efficiency of the FEC codec. For example, when there are 4 packet losses in one block, no matter whether these losses are consecutive or separated in the block, as long as there are 4 additional FEC packets in the same FEC block, the client would be able to recover these packet losses. Therefore, Hairpin does not rely on the assumption of underlying loss patterns but only focuses on the number of lost packets. Packet losses might be consecutive across several frames. In this case, due to the short feedback loop enabled by edge deployments, Hairpin should have already timely reacted as analyzed in §3.4.

5 Limitations

Delay components in interactive streaming Hairpin could have maximum benefits when the end-to-end network delay dominates the total delay from the video encoder to the decoder. This is generally true in interactive streaming services. Related measurement studies also demonstrate that the network delay is still one of the bottlenecks of edge-based interactive streaming [24, 40]. Therefore, we focus on optimizing streams between edge servers and clients. Our deployments in the wild demonstrate that optimizing the network latency could significantly improve the user's experience (note that DMR is measured end-to-end). Hairpin can also work with the optimization of other delay components (e.g., encoding, decoding, etc.) to further improve the performance.

Deployment efforts for applications Another concern of deploying Hairpin is that both the server and the client need modification to support the redundancy and retransmissions. There are previous efforts implementing the FEC mechanism over TCP [41, 42], which need to modify the TCP protocol stack at the client and are not suitable for products at scale. For scenarios where TCP is compulsory for transport, the deployment of Hairpin may depend on the ability to modify the reception mechanism of TCP packets at the client. However, most interactive streaming applications adopt UDP to reduce the network delay [43–46], including our service. In this case, Hairpin could be implemented within the application at the server and the client, which is practical for most applications.

6 Summary

We propose Hairpin, a packet loss recovery mechanism for edge-based interactive streaming to jointly optimize redundancy and retransmissions. Hairpin motivates the joint optimization with real-world measurements and optimizes the redundancy and retransmissions with the Markov decision process.

Try it out!
The implementation codes of Hairpin are available at https://github.com/hkust-spark/hairpin.

References

1. Winstein, K., Sivaraman, A., Balakrishnan, H.: Stochastic forecasts achieve high throughput and low delay over cellular networks. In: Proc, USENIX NSDI (2013)
2. Carlucci, G., De Cicco, L., Holmer, S., Mascolo, S.: Congestion control for web real-time communication. IEEE/ACM Trans. Netw. (2017)
3. Zhu, X., Pan, R., Ramalho, M., Mena, S.: Network-assisted dynamic adaptation (NADA): a unified congestion control scheme for real-time media. IETF RFC 8698 (2020)
4. Johansson, I., Sarker, Z.: Self-clocked rate adaptation for multimedia. IETF RFC 8298, (2017)
5. Arun, V., Balakrishnan, H.: Copa: Practical delay-based congestion control for the internet. In Proc, USENIX NSDI (2018)
6. Dong, M., Meng, T., Zarchy, D., Arslan, E., Gilad, Y., Godfrey, B., Schapira, M.: Pcc vivace: Online-learning congestion control. In Proc, USENIX NSDI (2018)
7. Holmer, S., Shemer, M., Paniconi, M.: Handling packet loss in webrtc. In: 2013 IEEE international conference on image processing (2013)
8. Emara, S., Fong, S.L., Li, B., Khisti, A., Tan, W. T., Zhu, X., Apostolopoulos, J.: Low-latency network-adaptive error control for interactive streaming. In: Proc. ACM Multimedia (2019)
9. Rudow, M., Yan, F.Y., Kumar, A., Ananthanarayanan, G., Ellis, M., Rashmi, K.V.: Streammelt: efficient loss recovery for videoconferencing via streaming codes. In: Proc. USENIX NSDI, 2023
10. Cheng, Y., Cardwell, N., Dukkipati, N., Jha, P.: The RACK-TLP loss detection algorithm for TCP. IETF RFC 8985 (2021)
11. Meng, Z., Kong, X., Chen, J., Wang, B., Xu, M., Han, R., Liu, H., Arun, V., Hu, H., Wei, X.: Hairpin: rethinking packet loss recovery in edge-based interactive video streaming. In: Proc, USENIX NSDI (2024)
12. Padhye, J., Firoiu, V., Towsley, D.F., Kurose, J.F.: Modeling tcp reno performance: a simple model and its empirical validation. IEEE/ACM Trans. Networking 8(2), 133–145 (2000)
13. Ha, S., Rhee, I., Xu, L.: Cubic: a new tcp-friendly high-speed tcp variant. ACM SIGOPS Operating Syst. Rev. (2008)
14. Cardwell, N., Cheng, Y., Gunn, C.S., Yeganeh, S.H., Jacobson, V.: Congestion-based congestion control. ACM Queue, Bbr (2016)

15. Zaki, Y., Pötsch, T., Chen, J., Subramanian, L., Görg, C.: Adaptive congestion control for unpredictable cellular networks. In Proc, ACM SIGCOMM (2015)
16. Garg, N.: Evaluating copa congestion control for improved video performance. https://engineering.fb.com/2019/11/17/video-engineering/copa/ (2019)
17. Sarolahti, P., Kojo, M., Raatikainen, K.: F-rto: an enhanced recovery algorithm for tcp retransmission timeouts. ACM SIGCOMM Comput. Commun. Rev. (2003)
18. Bolot, J.-C., Fosse-Parisis, S., Towsley, D.: Adaptive fec-based error control for internet telephony. In: Proc, IEEE INFOCOM (1999)
19. Padhye, C., Christensen, K.J., Moreno, W.: A new adaptive fec loss control algorithm for voice over ip applications. In: Proc. IEEE INFOCOM (2000)
20. Issue 93006: Update to media_opt_util: - code review. https://webrtc-codereview.appspot.com/93006 (2020)
21. Chen, K., Wang, H., Fang, S., Li, X., Ye, M., Jonathan Chao, H.: Rl-afec: adaptive forward error correction for real-time video communication based on reinforcement learning. In: Proc. ACM MMSys (2022)
22. Fong, Silas L., Khisti, A., Li, B., Tan, W.-T., Zhu, X., Apostolopoulos, J.: Optimal streaming codes for channels with burst and arbitrary erasures. IEEE Trans. Inform. Theory (2019)
23. Krishnan, M.N., Shukla, D., Kumar, P.V.: Rate-optimal streaming codes for channels with burst and random erasures. IEEE Trans. Inform. Theory (2020)
24. Meng, Z., Wang, T., Shen, Y., Wang, B., Xu, M., Han, R., Liu, H., Arun, V., Hu, H., Wei, X.: Enabling high quality real-time communications with adaptive frame-rate. In Proc, USENIX NSDI (2023)
25. Zhang, X., Chen, H., Zhao, Y., Ma, Z., Xu, Y., Huang, H., Yin, H., Wu, D.O.: Improving cloud gaming experience through mobile edge computing. IEEE Wireless Commun. (2019)
26. China Mobile and ZTE. Powered by sa: 5g mec-based cloud game innovation practice. GSMA 5G Case Studies (https://www.gsma.com/futurenetworks/wp-content/uploads/2020/03/Powered-by-SA-5G-MEC-Based-Cloud-Game-Innovation-Practice-.pdf), 2020
27. Carrascosa, M., Bellalta, B.: Cloud-gaming: Analysis of google stadia traffic. Comput. Commun. **188**, 99–116 (2022)
28. Kaarmukilan S.P. What is hairpin net shot in badminton? - quora. https://www.quora.com/What-is-hairpin-net-shot-in-badminton/answer/Kaarmukilan-S-P (2020)
29. Wiering, M.A., Van Otterlo, M.: Reinforcement learning and markov decision processes, pp. 3–42. Springer Berlin Heidelberg, Berlin, Heidelberg (2012)
30. Schwarz, H., Marpe, D., Wiegand, T.: Overview of the scalable video coding extension of the h. 264/avc standard. IEEE Trans. Circ. Syst. Video Technol. (2007)
31. Psa: Webrtc m88 release notes. https://groups.google.com/g/discuss-webrtc/c/A0FjOcTW2c0/m/UAv-veyPCAAJ (2020)
32. Ball, M., Navok, J.: Challenge #3: Enormous bandwidth costs and operational burdens | cloud gaming: Why it matters and the games it will create. https://www.matthewball.vc/all/cloudmiles (2020)
33. Haq, O., Raja, M., Dogar, Fahad R.: Measuring and improving the reliability of wide-area cloud paths. In: Proc. WWW (2017)
34. Chen, W., Ma, L., Shen, C.C.: Congestion-aware mac layer adaptation to improve video teleconferencing over wi-fi. In Proc, ACM MMSys (2015)
35. Lacan, J., Roca, V., Peltotalo, J., Peltotalo, S.: Reed-Solomon Forward Error Correction (FEC) Schemes. IETF RFC 5510 (2009)
36. Roca, V., Cunche, M., Lacan, J., Bouabdallah, A., Matsuzono, K.: Simple reed-solomon forward error correction (FEC) Scheme for FECFRAME. IETF RFC 6865 (2013)
37. Zanaty, M., Singh, V., Begen, A., Mandyam, G.: RTP payload format for flexible forward error correction (FEC). IETF RFC 8627 (2019)
38. Jain, M., Dovrolis, C.: End-to-end available bandwidth: measurement methodology, dynamics, and relation with tcp throughput. In: Proc, ACM SIGCOMM (2002)
39. Finite element method - wikipedia. https://en.wikipedia.org/wiki/Finite_element_method, 2021

40. Ghoshal, M., Dash, P., Kong, Z., Xu, Q., Charlie Hu, Y., Koutsonikolas, D., Li, Y.: Can 5g mmwave enable multi-user ar apps? In: Proc. PAM (2022)
41. Baldantoni, L., Lundqvist, H., Karlsson, G.: Adaptive end-to-end fec for improving tcp performance over wireless links. In: Proc, IEEE ICC (2004)
42. FFlach, T., Dukkipati, N., Terzis, A., Raghavan, B., Cardwell, N., Cheng, Y., Jain, A., Hao, S., Katz-Bassett, E., Govindan, R.: Reducing web latency: the virtue of gentle aggression. In: Proc, ACM SIGCOMM (2013)
43. Di Domenico, A., Perna, G., Trevisan, M., Vassio, L., Giordano, D.: A network analysis on cloud gaming: Stadia, geforce now and psnow. Network (2021)
44. Marczak, B., Scott-Railton, J.: Move fast and roll your own crypto: a quick look at the confidentiality of zoom meetings - the citizen lab. https://citizenlab.ca/2020/04/move-fast-roll-your-own-crypto-a-quick-look-at-the-confidentiality-of-zoom-meetings/ (2020)
45. brianhu. Google meet troubleshooting playbook - network and hardware troubleshooting. https://www.googlecloudcommunity.com/gc/Workspace-Product-Articles/Google-Meet-Troubleshooting-Playbook-Network-and-Hardware/ta-p/165810 (2021)
46. Rowe, C., Hanson, D., Craig, C., Coulter, D., Gilmore, J., Byrd, D., Borys, A., Baker, K., Hermansen, B., Soysal, S., et al.: Microsoft teams call flows - microsoft teams | microsoft docs. https://docs.microsoft.com/en-us/microsoftteams/microsoft-teams-online-call-flows (2021)

Chapter 7
Network Layer on Data Path: Smooth Queue Management

Abstract This chapter delves into the challenges and solutions related to managing network layer congestion to ensure low-latency interactive multimedia streaming. It reviews various approaches, including Active Queue Management (AQM), queue size optimization, and end-to-end message passing. The discussion highlights the difficulties in deploying these solutions, especially in wide-area networks. Emphasis is placed on the need for proactive strategies to mitigate latency fluctuations caused by flow competition. The chapter introduces a novel method, Confucius, to manage router queues and maintain consistent bandwidth for multimedia streaming, addressing the root causes of network-induced stalls and performance degradation.

Keywords Interactive multimedia streaming, Active queue management, Queue scheduling, Network layer latency, Congestion control

1 Network Layer Research Efforts on Data Path

In recent years, there has not been much optimization work on the network layer in wide-area networks. The main reason is that the main component of the network layer is routers within the network. In other scenarios, such as data centers, routers (or switches) are replaced more frequently. Therefore, new technologies have the opportunity for faster deployment. However, in wide-area networks, there is almost no situation where a single entity controls all devices on a path. Therefore, in the following discussion, the deployability of these works is an important point we focus on (Table 1).

On routers, they can operate the packets passing through the router to implicitly or explicitly inform the sender of the current network status. Based on this, the sender can be implicitly informed by active queue management techniques to achieve low latency—when the network status deteriorates, the router can selectively discard some packets. It can also directly adjust the queue size to limit its maximum latency physically—if the buffer is too small, packets have to be discarded. In this case, although the packet loss rate may increase, the latency can also be bounded, which is not necessarily a bad thing for real-time multimedia. Alternatively, new network

© The Author(s), under exclusive license to Springer Nature Singapore Pte Ltd. 2024   109
Z. Meng and M. Xu, *Latency Optimization in Interactive Multimedia Streaming*,
SpringerBriefs in Computer Science, https://doi.org/10.1007/978-981-97-6729-8_7

Table 1 Real-time multimedia optimization related work in the network layer

Academic/industry proposals	Solutions	Main ideas
CoDel (CACM'12) [1] RED[2], BLUE[3], GREEN[4], Yellow[5]	Active Queue Management	Drop packets early to force the sender to slow down to avoid over-sending
BDP/n (SIGMETRICS'21) [6] ABS (INFOCOM'22) [7]	Queue Size Optimization	Set appropriate queue size to reduce latency
XCP (SIGCOMM'02) [8] RCP (INFOCOM'08) [9] Kickass (ICNP'16) [10] ABC (NSDI'20) [11]	End-to-End Message Passing	Carry more dimensions of network state for better decision-making

layer protocols can be explicitly constructed to carry network status information back to the sender for information delivery purposes. This section will review these works from these perspectives.

1.1 Active Queue Management

In the network layer, Active Queue Management (AQM) is a common method to control network congestion. There are many AQM algorithms on routers. The earlier active queue management algorithm is RED [12], which informs the current network deterioration by probabilistically random dropping at an early stage. The default active queue management algorithm currently deployed on many edge routers is CoDel, proposed in 2012 [1], which mainly solves the problem that estimating queue length is difficult to adapt to routers with different bandwidths while using the dwell time in the queue can more accurately control the latency target. In addition, many more AQM algorithms have been proposed, such as SFB [13], Green [4], Yellow [5], Black [14], and AFD [15]. The latest development is the DualQ algorithm, which has just become an IETF RFC in 2023 [16] and is part of the IETF's L4S working group and performs active queue management by classifying data streams into different categories.

In addition, in data centers, there is a large amount of work to be done to manage the queues of data center switches. Examples include PIAS [17], pFabric [18], and ABM [19]. However, the biggest difference between these works and active queue management in wide-area networks is that they can assume cooperation between end hosts: an enterprise can control both switches and servers within its data center. This provides great convenience for flow type differentiation, flow size estimation, etc. However, on the Internet, we cannot make such assumptions. If an algorithm prioritizes a certain type of traffic, all Internet users will disguise their traffic as this type of traffic, rendering the mechanism ineffective. In fact, this is one of the reasons why mechanisms such as differentiated services[20] are less widely used in wide-area networks.

In comparison, they also have a common problem of assuming that the end-to-end congestion control algorithm is sensitive to packet loss or ECN marking. However, with the emergence of rate-based or delay-based congestion control algorithms such as Copa and BBR, they are no longer sensitive to packet loss or ECN. Therefore, if it is expected to rely on packet loss to reduce the sending rate of the end-to-end congestion control algorithm, this requires very serious packet loss. For example, BBR will not reduce the sending rate even when packet loss rates are up to 20%. Therefore, there is an urgent need to optimize new active queue management mechanisms for such delay-sensitive congestion control algorithms.

1.2   Queue Size Optimization

How to set the bottleneck queue size has always been a difficult problem in network layer management. A small queue can lead to frequent packet loss in the network when dealing with bursty traffic. A large queue, on the other hand, can cause long queuing delays when the rate adjustment is not timely. Therefore, setting the appropriate queue size has always been a concern for network administrators and an important means to reduce end-to-end latency. In this regard, there have been a series of empirical works exploring this issue. For example, in 2019, the Buffer Sizing Workshop organized by Stanford discussed how to set switch queue sizes. In addition, there are many adaptive queue size works, such as ABS [7]. It adjusts the router's queue size adaptively based on the burstiness of network traffic.

Another major work in queue size optimization is theoretical analysis. Decades ago, an analysis demonstrated that the bottleneck queue size should be no less than the Bandwidth-Delay Product (BDP). This will ensure that the congestion control algorithms at that time (e.g., AIMD or Vegas) could fully utilize the link capacity [21]. Subsequently, in 2004, [22] proposed that by utilizing the statistical multiplexing characteristics of different congestion control flows, the bottleneck queue size can be reduced to $BDP/\sqrt{N}$, where N is the number of flows on the switch. In recent years, researchers have pointed out that with the emergence of new congestion control algorithms such as BBR, the bottleneck queue size can be further reduced to BDP/N [6]. As a result, the maximum possible latency on the switch may also continue to decrease.

However, this setting only applies to core backbone switches, as they typically have millions of flows. In edge routers (e.g., home wireless routers), there may be only tens or hundreds of flows in most cases. In this case, since N is small, the result is actually trivial. A more drastic issue is that in wireless networks, as described in Chapter 1, the bandwidth can be extremely fluctuating, so operators have to set a long queue. This leads to the situation where many last-hop routers have very "deep" queue buffers. In this case, the occurrence of high latency is difficult to avoid. The work in this chapter is trying to shorten the end-to-end latency without changing this setting.

1.3 End-to-End Message Passing

The last category of work is to design new protocols at the network layer to better communicate between end hosts and network devices. Having good message passing can also conveniently control latency since the end host can strictly follow the changes in available bandwidth. Consequently, there will be no congestion due to improper self-adjustment. Typical work in this area is XCP in 2002 [8] and subsequent RCP [9]. They design new protocols that include the bottleneck bandwidth rate in the protocol header fields to control the sending rate precisely. This also includes some works that may not have designed new protocols but have similarly carried network status information in existing protocols, such as Kickass [10] and ABC [11]. Kickass [10] passes the available bandwidth information of a flow on the current router back to the sender through the size of IP fragments. ABC [11] uses the two bits left over from differentiated services (TOS) that are not widely used on the Internet to mark whether the current router thinks the flow needs to speed up or slow down.

However, the biggest problem with these works is still the lack of deployability. There are numerous innovations in the network layer, but very few have been truly deployed in the Internet. The main reason is that it is extremely difficult to modify network devices. The above schemes require modifications to both network devices and end host devices. This is very difficult in practice: end host devices are usually maintained by content providers (such as Google and Netflix); while network devices are maintained by device vendors (such as Cisco and Netgear). Coordinating between both parties to make changes to achieve performance gains has been proven to be very difficult in the long history of Internet development—see the endless debates in IETF meetings.

In this chapter, we always adhere to the principle of minimizing modifications to devices. The proposed work can be deployed with benefits by modifying only a single network device without the need for communication and collaboration with other devices. In this way, the work is deployable to some extent and has some examples of actual deployment in the current network.

2   Introduction

Significant research has been dedicated to ensuring a satisfactory user experience by minimizing and stabilizing end-to-end latency. Indeed, congestion control algorithms (CCAs) reduce the queueing delay [23–25]; forward error correction (FEC) improves the loss recovery [26, 27]; multiple path transport mitigates fluctuation in wireless settings [28–30]; while co-design with the video codec [31, 32] and wire-

Fig. 1 The scenario where the interactive multimedia streaming flow is affected by competing flows. When Web flows join the competition with the interactive multimedia streaming flow, the available bandwidth of the interactive multimedia streaming flow will be immediately reduced. Note that even loading one Web page can have tens of concurrent active flows

less routers [33, 34] controls the delay in these components. Unfortunately, these works mainly *focus on how to mitigate the effect of network fluctuations after the fact, instead of addressing their root cause.* As a result, latency fluctuations still routinely occur, causing stalls and deterioration of the performance of the interactive multimedia streaming flow [35, 36].

This chapter shows that unpredictable flow competition in the network layer can cause drastic network fluctuation, drastically affecting interactive multimedia streaming flows (§3). For instance, loading a single Web page creates nine concurrent Internet connections (on average), drastically reducing the available bandwidth for the competing interactive multimedia streaming flows and causing stalls in multiple practical settings such as home routers, as shown in Fig. 1. Congestion control alleviates the issue by reducing the interactive multimedia streaming flow's congestion window or sending rate after end hosts observe latency increases or packet loss, but it is already far too late. Indeed, it will take several RTTs for congestion control to react and converge to the new available bandwidth, while the *packets sent in excess of the allocated bandwidth* during the convergence period will lead to an increase in the end-to-end delay. These endpoint-based optimizations, in general, cannot fundamentally prevent such performance degradation from happening since the onset of competing traffic is unpredictable.

A natural solution to flow competition is to manage the router queue and prevent the available bandwidth of the interactive multimedia streaming flow from reducing. There have been works trying to achieve this for several decades. In differentiated services (DiffServ) [20], including L4S [37], the router recognizes the pre-defined labels (priorities) from packet headers and schedules packets based on these labels. However, such a design is not incentive-compatible in practice: applications have the incentive to mark their packets with higher priority, which eventually leads to the Tragedy of Commons—routers will not respect the labels, and endpoints cannot count on using them. Another category of solutions on the router is Active Queue Management (AQM), which tries to notify the sender in advance before the queue builds up [1, 2, 33]. We demonstrate in §3 that these are still reactive mechanisms and cannot prevent stalls from happening.

The root cause for stalls in the interactive multimedia streaming flows from the network layer perspective is the *mismatch in reaction time between the bandwidth allocation mechanisms on routers and rate adaptation mechanisms on endpoints.* In

Fig. 1, when nine new flows triggered by a single website (in yellow) suddenly compete with an existing interactive multimedia streaming flow (in blue), the available bandwidth of the interactive multimedia streaming flow is *immediately* reduced to 1/10 of what it was. However, the sender's congestion window needs several round-trip times (RTTs) to gradually adjust to match the new available bandwidth. During this adjustment period, packets that are sent in excess of the allocated bandwidth will induce congestion, resulting in bufferbloat and stalls. While the Web flows will complete within one or two seconds and relinquish their bandwidth share, the interactive multimedia streaming flow will have already experienced significant degradation. We find that existing queue scheduling and management algorithms *ignore the transient temporal behaviors during the network change*, leading to stalls. This highlights a critical need for a queue management scheme that takes into account the convergence time of the congestion control to prevent such stalls.

To this end, we presented Confucius[1], a practical queue management scheme that aims at providing consistent low latency for interactive multimedia streaming flows independently of competing flows at the bottleneck. Instead of abruptly changing bandwidth allocations when a burst of new flows arrives, Confucius *gradually* adjusts the service rates to provide existing flows a few RTTs to detect the change in network conditions and adjust their congestion windows. In this case, the excessively sent packets will be reduced, and the latency of the interactive multimedia streaming flow will be maintained.

Confucius fulfills three fundamental requirements related to consistency, fairness and incentive compatibility (§4.1): First, Confucius needs to provide latency consistency to interactive multimedia streaming flows independently of the number, rate, or congestion control of the competing flows. Confucius achieves this by offering a theoretical upper bound for latency fluctuation experienced by interactive multimedia streaming flows, which we also validate through experiments Second, Confucius should eventually be fair. For instance, in §1, the performance of Web flows should not be sacrificed. To achieve this, Confucius smoothly moves service rates toward the fair allocation within a few RTTs. Finally, Confucius's classification of interactive multimedia streaming flow should be practical and on-router without relying on end hosts for traffic classification. Unfortunately, the alternative—flow classification algorithms—are usually expensive and sensitive to protocols [38]. Confucius classifies flows by *how aggressively they occupy the buffer* at the bottleneck router, a metric that directly reflects how important low latency is to a flow.

3   Motivation

We start by describing recent trends that call for consistent low latency (§3.1). Next, we explain via an intuitive example why existing solutions fail to achieve consistent low latency under flow competition (§3.2, 3.3, 3.4).

---

[1] Confucius' (the philosopher) educational philosophy is teaching students by their essences. In this paper, we serve the flows by their essences.

3.1   The Rise of Real-Time Traffic

While the Internet has always been shared among multiple applications, the proliferation of real-time communication applications (*e.g.,* videoconferencing, cloud gaming, virtual reality) has made sharing of bottleneck links particularly challenging. Real-time applications require not just low latency but *consistently* low latency while sending at moderate to high throughputs (ranging from tens to hundreds of Mbps) [33, 39, 40]. For real-time applications, latency consistency is extremely critical to user experiences. For example, a transient increase in latency to 200 ms might cause cloud gaming users to lose [41]. Therefore, controlling the latency fluctuation and achieving a consistent low latency for real-time applications is essential.

Setting & Scope: This work focuses on end-user access points (*e.g.,* wireless or wired home routers), where it is well-known that congestion and latency fluctuation are frequent [33, 42, 43]. Despite recent advances in wireless technologies such as 5G and WiFi 6, the last-mile access routers are still likely to be the cause of jitter, irrespective of whether the last-mile is wired [44] or wireless [33, 45, 46]. As most such routers are Linux-based [47, 48], they allow for flexible traffic management on software which is a great opportunity for innovation. Our experiments and data involve applications used in those settings. Congestion in other settings (*e.g.,* losses in the Internet core [49] or datacenters [17]) are out of scope for this work.

3.2   Motivating Example

To better illustrate the problem and the limitations of existing approaches, we revisit the example of Fig. 1 in detail. Consider a user who is on a video call, and their housemate (with whom they share the home router) decides to load a Web page. Technically, one existing interactive multimedia streaming flow on the bottleneck will compete with the new flows from one Web page. We simulate the interactive multimedia streaming flow's delay of each video frame using NS-3 and present the results in Fig. 2 (details in §7). Before considering other queue management mechanisms, let us focus on the performance of FIFO (square markers).

Before t=0 s, the sending rate of the interactive multimedia streaming flow has converged, with the video frame delay fluctuating around 60ms, which is much lower than the stall threshold (190ms[2]) required by the application. However, when flows from loading the homepage of www.amazon.com join the competition on the bottleneck, the end-to-end delay for the interactive multimedia streaming flow sharply increases. Using FIFO, the delay goes up to more than 400 ms, and stays above the threshold for almost one second, during which a stall occurs and the user experience is impaired. When using FqCoDel, the delay of the interactive multimedia streaming flow is even worse since fair queueing shifts more bandwidth away and CoDel drops more packets. The delay *always* spikes regardless of the underlying CCA.

---

[2] This is the recommended network delay for video chats by ITU [50].

3.3 Root Cause Analysis

We argue that the delay spike is caused by (i) the burst of flows and packets from the competing Web page; (ii) the abrupt reallocation of the available bandwidth by queue management; and (iii) the gradual reaction from the congestion control. Next, we will elaborate on how these common factors result in performance degradation, and explain the limitations of existing works.

The source of the burst: One Web page triggers multiple, concurrently active flows. To understand the burst in Fig. 2, we measure the flows triggered by https://amazon.com over time. Concretely, we measure the number of sockets that are OPEN and IN_USE marked by NetLog [51] from Chrome. We also measure the number of active flows that receive bytes every 10 ms through packet captures (ACTIVE). As shown in Fig. 3, loading only the homepage generates up to 68 flows in total, where up to 12 flows run simultaneously. This is due to the Web design of hosting different objects (*e.g.,* images, videos, ads, scripts) in various domains. Note that this is not due to the parallel connections in HTTP/1.1—more than half of the flows go to different unique IPs.

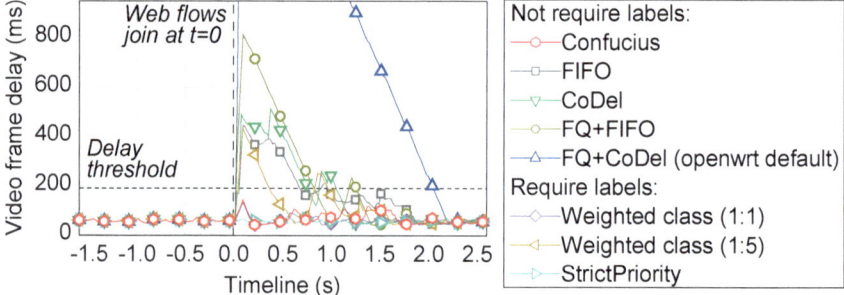

Fig. 2 An existing interactive multimedia streaming flow competes with flows of loading the homepage of www.amazon.com, as shown in Fig. 1. The interactive multimedia streaming flow, using GCC [23], always experiences transient stalls during the competition unless flows are pre-labeled by the end host and differentiated by the router

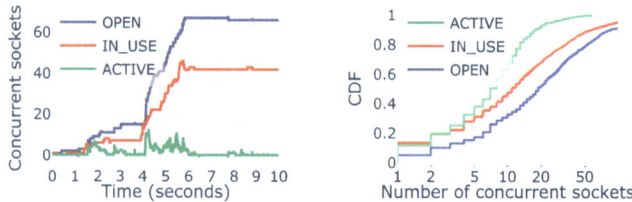

Fig. 3 Number of *concurrent* flows recorded by NetLog [51], with the timeline of an example, https://amazon.com (**left**) and the distribution of all websites (**right**). OPEN and IN_USE are socket states marked by Chrome, and ACTIVE means that the flow is receiving bytes in the last 10 ms

This triggering of multiple flows to load one page is shared across different websites. We measured the homepage of Top 1000 websites in November 2023 from the saved Alexa list and presented the distribution in Fig. 3. We find that the median number of concurrent `ACTIVE` flows is 8 while the 90th percentile is 19. The highest one in the Top 200, https://dailymail.co.uk, has up to 50 active flows and 250 open sockets at the same time. Moreover, for some websites (*e.g.*, Wikipedia and Google), loading other pages triggers more flows compared to the almost blank home page, which will further exacerbate the degradation experienced by the interactive multimedia streaming flow.

The cause of the delay spike: Queue schedulers sharply reallocate service rates. Queue management typically reacts to the instant conditions of all flows in the queue. Revisiting our example, when the page loading starts, tens of packets of Web flows immediately arrive at the bottleneck, creating a queue. At the same time, the interactive multimedia streaming flow only has a few packets in the queue since it always tries to keep the queue near-empty [23, 25]. We illustrate the bandwidth share of different queue management schemes in Fig. 4. For `FIFO` (Fig. 4a), the service rates for different flows are proportional to the number of bytes per-flow in the queue, thus, the available bandwidth for the interactive multimedia streaming flow will be drastically reduced. Fair queueing (`FQ`, Fig. 4b) makes matters worse and allocates even less bandwidth to the interactive multimedia streaming flow, since those short Web flows are many more than the interactive multimedia streaming flow. Concretely, in the https://amazon.com example, 12 new flows joining the fair queueing router will directly reduce the available bandwidth of the interactive multimedia streaming flow to 1/13.

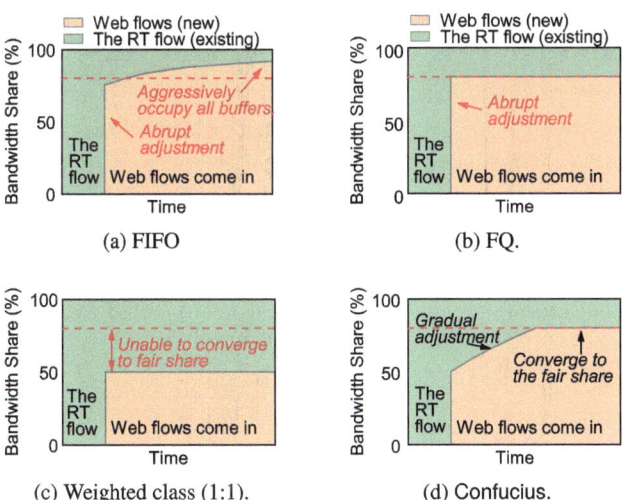

Fig. 4 Illustration of how bandwidth shares change over time with incoming Web flows and the existing real-time (RT) flow for different schedulers. The dashed red line marks the fair share

Such a sharp decrease in the available bandwidth causes a delay spike to the interactive multimedia streaming flow. This is because the CCA needs to *gradually* probe and match its sending rate to the new available bandwidth, which takes several RTTs (dashed green line in Fig. 5). While the number of in-flight packets is converging to the new bandwidth-delay product, the excessive in-flight packets will cause bufferbloat and result in high end-to-end latency for the interactive multimedia streaming flow.

Active queue management (AQM) algorithms, which notify the sender about the network conditions by dropping or marking ECN on packets, cannot prevent stalls either. This is mainly because flows driven by different congestion control algorithms (CCAs) have different perceptions of congestion (*e.g.,* delay, loss, rate). Therefore, as shown in Fig. 2, CoDel [1] leads to a latency spike even higher than that of FIFO. Similar limitations can also be observed in other AQMs [52].

The fact hard to change: Congestion control takes a longer time to converge. As we discussed, the issue is when the competing flows join, the available bandwidth for the interactive multimedia streaming flow drops immediately, but the end-to-end CCA cannot immediately reduce the in-flight packets to fit the new available bandwidth. End-to-end CCAs do not know how much to reduce and have to reduce step-by-step.

Some proposals are designed to help the CCA to quickly converge to the new available bandwidth, such as XCP [8], RCP [9], Kickass [10], and ABC [11]. However, none of these proposals work unless both end hosts and routers collaboratively deploy these protocols and offer no improvement otherwise. This poses significant barriers to deployment on the Internet [33]. Moreover, during the convergence of the CCA, the excessive in-flight packets also inflate the RTT. For most CCAs using RTT to update (*e.g.,* adjust the sending rate every RTT), the update period will, in turn, inflate after the first several packets. In the example in Fig. 2, before the Web flows join, the RTT for the interactive multimedia streaming flow is around 40 ms. However, during the competition, the RTT inflates to hundreds of milliseconds. Putting all factors together, we can see that for all baselines that do not require labels, the delay spike of the interactive multimedia streaming flow goes up to at least 400 ms.

Fig. 5 When new competing flows join, the service rate of the interactive multimedia streaming flow will be immediately reduced, but the CCA takes multiple RTTs to converge

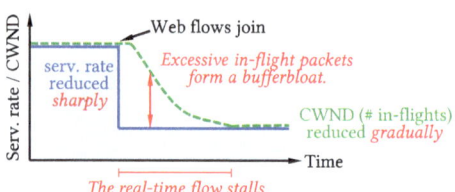

3.4   Limitations of Related Works

One line of solution is DiffServ [20], which labels the flows of interest in advance and schedules them differently on the router using `StrictPriority` or `weighted class` as shown in Fig. 2. This also includes the recent proposal L4S [37]. While this is deployable in datacenters [53], it is not practical on the Internet. End hosts have the incentive to fake their labels if that could help their flows have better performance. It is also challenging to coordinate the end host and router on the Internet in the real world since they usually belong to different entities. Even with perfect labels, achieving optimal performance requires optimal allocation of bandwidth across the different classes of traffic. To understand why this is challenging, consider some canonical solutions. `StrictPriority`, albeit guaranteeing the latency for the interactive multimedia streaming flow, will drastically harm the performance of competing Web flows [52]. Allocating bandwidth for different classes using pre-defined weights needs accurate estimation of the bandwidth demands from both classes, where inaccurate estimation easily leads to unfairness or latency spikes. For example, if we set the ratio between the interactive multimedia streaming flows and Web flows to 1:1, the Web flows will suffer from degraded PLT since they cannot obtain their fair shares (Fig. 4c), while 1:5 will lead to the latency spike to the interactive multimedia streaming flow as well (Fig. 2).

There are further mechanisms as below, which, unfortunately, still reactively respond to network changes. Zhuge [33] reduces the feedback loop between the router and the endpoint from one RTT to sub-RTT levels, but CCA convergence still requires multiple RTTs (§3.3). Using the example in Fig. 5, Zhuge tightens the turning point of the green dashed line, but the dominant contributor to delay – the time it takes for the green dashed line to converge to the blue line – persists. FEC is designed for loss recovery [26, 27] and is hardly helpful in our example since most of them have no loss at all. Multipath transport will switch to the new path [29, 30, 54], but this also occurs *after* the sender observes drastic degradation in the current path. Interactive multimedia streaming flows still have to suffer from stalls during the adaptation period. Bandwidth estimations from the wireless link layer and below [33, 55] are not effective either since the link capacity does not change in the competition.

4   Confucius Design

Our previous observations motivate Confucius, a practical queue management scheme for achieving consistent and low latency for interactive multimedia streaming flows that are designed to work on home routers. We describe Confucius's design requirements in §4.1 before we give an overview of Confucius on §4.2.

4.1 Design Requirements

R1: The performance of the interactive multimedia streaming flow should be robust to any competing flows. Confucius stands out among queue management algorithms in that it theoretically guarantees worst-case performance, no matter what congestion control algorithms and competing flows are. This will, in consequence, fundamentally address the root cause of latency fluctuation induced by unpredictable competing traffic. It is easy to vaguely describe Confucius as 'controlling latency fluctuations', but it is harder to formulate this into a rigorous service model. We theoretically calculate performance bounds for a few classes of applications that might use Confucius. We demonstrate that with Confucius, interactive multimedia streaming flows have a near-constant bound of latency degradation (around 250 ms), no matter how large and how many competing flows join the bottleneck.

R2: Latency consistency should not come at the cost of long-term fairness. Confucius should still follow per-flow fairness in the long run. To do so, Confucius moves rates toward a fair allocation quickly and pushes the blue solid line in Fig. 5 to match the green dashed line. In this case, the latency spike will be controlled and the bandwidth for the competing flows will be largely protected as well. Technically, Confucius adjusts the service rate of flows using exponentially weighted moving average (EWMA) [56], as shown in Fig. 4d. This allows the CCA to gradually react following the bandwidth share of Confucius, and also converges to the fair share in several RTTs. Note that the RTT is not inflated due to the excessive packets. Such a design can effectively achieve fairness and latency consistency.

R3: The identification of interactive multimedia streaming flows should not rely on end hosts. A naive solution is to split the flows by their age. However, this is not practical since flows driven by different CCAs or having distinct objectives should not share the same queue either. Meanwhile, using FQ to split old flows cannot provide low latency to the bursty flows [57], which is usually the case for real-time video streaming. Thus, we still need to identify different types of flows. To make Confucius incentive-compatible and deployable in practice, we aim to identify the flows of interest *at the router itself*, without relying on end hosts. The performance improvements should be directly observed by the router vendor without going through endless coordination between end-host content providers and router vendors in IETF. In §6, we illustrate how Confucius identifies flows based on their queue occupancy: built on the CCA evolution, interactive multimedia streaming flows naturally occupy a small fraction of the buffer (e.g., GCC [23, 25]), while throughput-oriented flows are observed to be buffer-filling (e.g., Cubic). Confucius uses the queue occupancy to differentiate the flows in the queue.

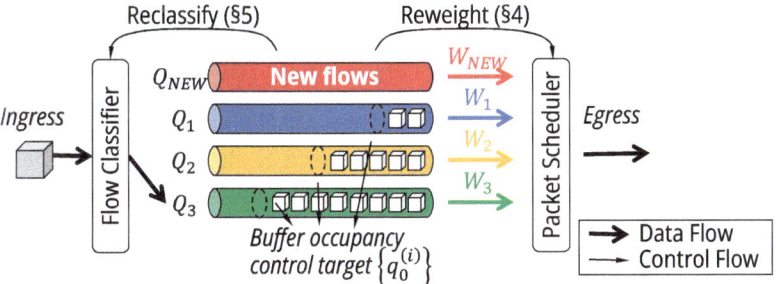

Fig. 6 Design overview of Confucius. w_i denotes the weight for queue i in the scheduling with DWRR

4.2 Design Overview

At a high level, Confucius classifies flows to queues and strategically assigns a portion of the link capacity to each of them, as illustrated in Fig. 6.

To address the goal **R1** and **R2**, Confucius leverages a simple yet powerful insight from §4.1: Upon the arrival of competitors, the reduction of the available bandwidth of existing flows is inevitable if we want to preserve long-term throughput fairness. Yet, we can gradually and cautiously control the reduction of the available bandwidth during the transient period. Thus, we can eliminate the mismatch between the sending rate of the CCA and the service rate at the bottleneck link for existing interactive multimedia streaming flows, thereby taming the latency fluctuation. We will extend our insight of using the EWMA reweight mechanism in §5.

For **R3**, by grouping flows with similar queue occupancy into the same queue, flows with different queue occupancies will not affect each other. Meanwhile, with a fixed number of queues to schedule between (instead of per-flow queues such as FQ), latency-sensitive flows will have a consistent latency. Thus, Confucius uses a set of queues (Q_1, Q_2, Q_3), each designed to accommodate old flows with different buffer occupancies, and a separate queue (Q_{NEW}) dedicated to new flows. It then adopts a Deficit-Weighted Round-Robin (DWRR) algorithm to schedule between these queues. Finally, Confucius periodically measures flow characteristics and reclassifies flows using a hysteresis-based mechanism to increase robustness in practice further (§6).

5 Age-Aware Flow Weights Adjustment

In this section, we explain the benefits of exponential bandwidth reallocation (§5.1) and dive into Confucius' weight adjustment (§5.2). We then analytically show that it guarantees bounded performance degradation, both for existing interactive multimedia streaming flows and newly-arrived competing flows (§5.3).

5.1   *Exponential Bandwidth Re-Allocation*

We first quantitatively demonstrate the advantage of *gradually* controlling the inter-active multimedia streaming flow's bandwidth allocation compared to directly cutting its available bandwidth to its fair share. We measured the stall duration y for the inter-active multimedia streaming flow in the scenario of a sudden reduction of available bandwidth for four low-latency CCAs (§5). Concretely, y denotes the stall duration defined by more than 190 ms of end-to-end delay. We plot y as a function of the *Available Bandwidth Reduction Factor* (ABRF, the factor we will reduce the avail-able bandwidth) for different CCAs in Fig. 7a. We find that CCAs respond poorly to sudden, large reductions in bandwidth. For instance, reducing GCC's available bandwidth to 1/16 of its initial value (i.e., $ABRF = 16$) results in a $y > 10\ seconds$ stall. The relationship between the stall duration and ABRF ($y = f_{CCA}(ABRF)$) is super-linear.

To avoid such stalls, Confucius *gradually* reduces the available bandwidth for the interactive multimedia streaming flow. For instance, to achieve a final ABRF of 16, we can reduce the available bandwidth four times, each by half. Figure 7b demonstrates, in the ideal case, the value proposition of this approach. Compared to the super-linear stall duration (solid line copied from Figure reffig:jitterspsreduca), exponentially reducing the sending rate will only increase the stall duration *logarithmically* with the ABRF (modulated by $f_{CCA}(2)$, a small constant).

Such a smooth reallocation of available bandwidth allows the CCA to learn the reduced bandwidth allocation and is also robust to the number or size of competing flows. No matter how many flows compete with the interactive multimedia streaming flow, the curve of the available bandwidth is fixed, so the delay will remain the same. Meanwhile, adjusting the bandwidth share exponentially yields fast convergence to the fair share, satisfying requirements **R1** and **R2** together. We prove in §5.3, that Confucius guarantees that the long-term fairness will not be impaired, and the

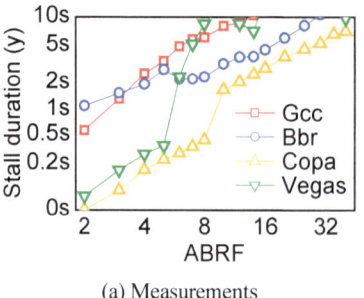

(a) Measurements

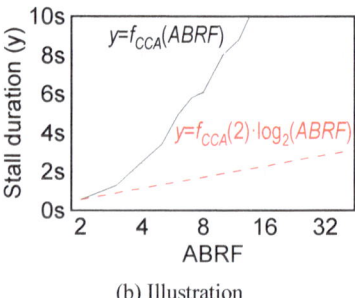

(b) Illustration

Fig. 7   a Stall duration increases with the available-bandwidth-reduction factor (ABRF). **b** An illustration of how gently reducing available bandwidth helps reduce delay duration. Note that **a** is a log-log plot, but **b** is a log-lin plot

degradation of the performance for new flows will *always be within a constant, additive factor* of the FCT under a strictly fair allocation.

5.2   Adjustment Mechanism

To assign service rates to queues, Confucius uses the following process. For each flow, f, Confucius computes a weight, w_f, to represent its share of the bandwidth (service rate). Confucius groups new flows into a separate queue called Q_{new} (depicted in Fig. 6). All existing flows which are mapped to other queues are assigned flow weights of $w_f = 1$, and are collectively denoted as set $\mathcal{F}_{ext}$. The flow weights of all flows in Q_{new} are computed as follows:

$$w_f = \min\left(\frac{|\mathcal{F}_{ext}|}{|Q_{new}|} \cdot 2^{\lambda t}, \ 1 \right), \quad f \in Q_{new} \tag{1}$$

Then, for a given queue, Q, the weight is the sum of weights of all flows in Q. There are several considerations in Eq. (1):

Age-aware exponential adjustment $(2^{\lambda t})$. As described in §4.1, Confucius *exponentially increases* the weights of new flows, where the bandwidth shares are illustrated in Figure 4d. Here, t represents the age (in milliseconds) of the new flow, and λ is a parameter that controls the speed for the rate adjustment of new flows—their flow weights double every $\frac{1}{\lambda}$ milliseconds. A large λ (e.g., $\lambda \to \infty$) leads to abrupt reductions in available bandwidth and causes latency spike, while a small λ (e.g., $\lambda = 0$) results in unfairness for new flows. Consequently, we configure λ so that the available bandwidth for the interactive multimedia streaming flow drops as fast as possible but not overtaking the responsiveness of the underlying CCAs.

Moreover, different CCAs have different response times to congestion. For example, Copa needs 5 RTTs to reduce its sending rate, while BBR's response time is dictated by its probing interval of 6–8 RTTs. To deal with the heterogeneity of CCAs on the Internet [58], we set λ as the inverse of *the response time of the least responsive CCA* among common latency-sensitive CCAs. This ensures that even the least responsive CCA can smoothly react to bandwidth changes. Recall that we measure how different CCAs respond to bandwidth reductions in Fig. 7a, which shows BBR being the least responsive CCA: When the ABRF is 2, BBR suffers from the longest stall compared with other CCAs due to its long probing period of 6–8 RTTs. Thus, given a typical RTT of 30–50 ms for Web services [59], we set λ=0.004 (ms^{-1}) to have a doubling interval of $\frac{1}{\lambda}$=250 ms, matching BBR's probing period.

Initial weight $\left(\frac{|\mathcal{F}_{ext}|}{|Q_{new}|} \right)$. To allocate sufficient share for new flows, we scale the initial weight of new flows with the *number of existing flows*. For each new flow, we set the initial weight to $\frac{|\mathcal{F}_{ext}|}{|Q_{new}|}$, where $|\mathcal{F}_{ext}|$ and $|Q_{new}|$ are the numbers of existing and new flows, respectively. This can limit the bandwidth reduction for existing flows to be less aggressive than a factor-of-2 reduction. In this case, the stall duration can logarithmically scale from $f_{CCA}(2)$, as shown in Fig. 7b.

Upper bound (min(..., 1)). Confucius uses a flow weight threshold of 1 to 'age out' new flows from the Q_{new} queue. Once the flow weight of a flow reaches 1, the flow is no longer considered new and is moved to one of the other queues based on the output of the Flow Classifier (§6).

5.3 *Theoretical Analysis*

We still follow the same example in §3.2. Consider one interactive multimedia streaming flow running by itself on a bottleneck link. At $t = 0$, N new flows, each with size B, join the same bottleneck link and compete with the existing flow. B_0 is the initial congestion window for Web flows. We show that Confucius guarantees a bounded stall for the existing interactive multimedia streaming flow while yielding FCTs for Web flows within a constant additive factor of what FQ provides. For simplicity, we summarize the results in Table 2 and leave the analytical details to [52].

For FQ and FIFO, we observe that the stall duration (q_P^{max}) scales linearly with the number of new flows, N, and is therefore unbounded, where N can go to more than 100 in some Web pages (Fig. 3). This is quite straightforward – when N flows start to compete with the interactive multimedia streaming flow, the available bandwidth of the interactive multimedia streaming flow drops to $1/N$. Intuitively, as N increases, the available bandwidth for the interactive multimedia streaming flow drops, resulting in drastic delay fluctuation.

For class-based queues (CBQ, weighted class), pre-labeling the interactive multimedia streaming flow enables the scheduler to allocate the interactive multimedia

Table 2 Approximations for different schedulers P on their maximum queueing delay (q_P^{max}) and FCT degradation against FQ ($T_P - T_{FQ}$)

Policy P	q_P^{max}	$T_P - T_{FQ}$
FQ	$\approx N\left(\frac{2}{3}\sqrt{\frac{2}{k}} + q_0 + \tau\right)$	0
FIFO	$\approx$ $\left(\frac{NB_0}{q_0 C} + 1\right)\left(\frac{2}{3}\sqrt{\frac{2}{k}} + q_0 + \tau\right)$	$\lesssim 0$
CBQ	$\approx \frac{2}{3}\sqrt{\frac{2}{k}} + q_0 + \tau$	$\approx \frac{(N-1)B}{C}$
Confucius	$\approx 6q_0 + 15\tau + \frac{8\lambda}{k} +$ $\frac{(10q_0+15\tau)\lambda^2}{k}$	$\approx \frac{\log_2 e}{\lambda}$

Confucius has a bounded performance degradation for all flows. In the competition, existing schedulers have either unbounded delay or unbounded FCT degradation. The unbounded terms with workload changes (N and B) are marked in red

streaming flow with a fixed bandwidth share, resulting in a constant stall. However, if the weights are not accurate (i.e., not matching the traffic ratio), CBQ converges unfairly, and the FCT degradation for new flows becomes unbounded (§3.4).

Finally, Confucius yields bounded performance degradation for *both sets of flows*. On one hand, Confucius ensures that the stall for interactive multimedia streaming flows is constant only depending on the CCA's latency sensitivity (denoted by q_0), the responsiveness (k), the feedback loop (τ), and Confucius's decay parameter $(\lambda)^3$. On the other hand, Confucius can also ensure the FCT degradation for new flows is bounded by an additive constant factor to the decay parameter (λ), which goes to negligible with the increase of the flow sizes.

6 Occupancy-Aware Flow Classification

As described in §4.2, Confucius seeks to classify flows into groups, each with a dedicated queue based on how aggressively they consume buffer space. *We find that flows implicitly demonstrate their preferences and objectives based on how they utilize the bottleneck queue.* We measure the buffer occupancy of 7 CCAs (the top-5 CCAs used in websites [58] plus two recent latency-sensitive CCAs, GCC, and Copa) over real-world bandwidth traces. We further measure the network RTT at the sender and the queue utilization on the bottleneck router. A lower RTT indicates that this CCA is more latency-sensitive. As we can see in Fig. 8, GCC, Copa, and Vegas have a low network RTT. Such CCAs achieve low latency by trying to keep the bottleneck queue as short as they can. Real-time applications can choose these CCAs to achieve low latency. In contrast, throughput-oriented CCAs (Cubic, Yeah, and Illinois) will maximize the queue utilization for high throughput. This allows us to identify the latency sensitivity of flows by their queue occupancy: if one flow has a low queue occupancy at the bottleneck, it indicates that (i) that flow tries to not overutilize the queue; and (ii) that flow can co-exist with other flows with similar behaviors.

Fig. 8 The relationship between queue utilization and delay in different CCAs. Experiments are simulated with real WiFi traces from [33]

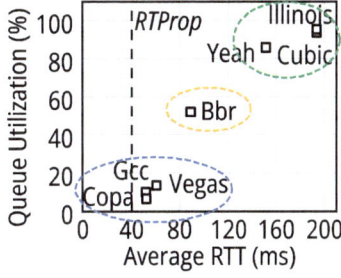

---

3 When using Copa with an RTT of 40ms, $q_{Confucius}^{max}$ is ≈640 ms. We show experimentally in [52] that the actual delay using Confucius is much lower.

In this section, we present our hysteresis-based mechanism to robustly identify the flows (§6.1) and our implementation considerations (§6.2).

6.1 Hysteresis-Based Adjustment

Confucius puts short flows into a separate queue Q_{new} and classifies long flows with different buffer occupancy aggressiveness into $Q_1, Q_2, \cdots, Q_n$. Queue indices increase with buffer target *i.e.,* Q_1 will be shorter than Q_3, as shown in Fig. 6. Each queue Q_i targets a buffer occupancy of $q_0^{(i)}$. We robustly classify flows as follows:

Classification of new flows. The buffer aggressiveness of flow may take a long time to manifest. Thus, Confucius will not characterize short flows lasting only a few RTTs (§3). When the new flow is ready to be moved out from the new flow queue Q_{new} to one of the old queues (its weight reaching one, which we elaborated on in §5.2), we measure the buffer occupancy of that flow q_f *i.e.,* the number of packets of this queue that belong to flow f. We then find the queue i with the nearest target $q_0^{(i)}$ to accommodate this flow.

Periodic adaptation. Confucius periodically examines flows and queues and moves flows accordingly in two steps. While seemingly complex, these operations are well within the capabilities of Linux-based routers (§7).

Intra-queue examination identifies outstanding flows among other flows in the current queue. Confucius examines the buffer each flow occupies ($\frac{q_f}{\sum_{g \in Q_i} q_g}$) and its fair share ($\frac{1}{|Q_i|}$). If the buffer occupancy of a flow is larger than its fair share:

$$\frac{q_f}{\sum_{g \in Q_i} q_g} \geqslant \frac{1}{|Q_i|} + \alpha \qquad (2)$$

the flow is too aggressive in the current queue, where $\alpha > 0$ is a hysteresis. Confucius wll promote that flow from queue Q_i to Q_{i+1} to keep Q_i near its control target. Similarly, a flow with an outstandingly lower buffer occupancy, i.e.:

$$\frac{q_f}{\sum_{f \in Q_i} q_f} \leqslant \frac{1}{|Q_i|} - \alpha \qquad (3)$$

will be demoted from queue Q_i to Q_{i-1}. Here we set α to 10% based on our previous observations in Fig. 8.

Queue-level examination checks if the length of a queue fits the queue's control target. If the length of a queue exceeds a safe region between the control target of the neighbor queue, Confucius moves all flows in the current queue to that queue, as shown in Fig. 9. This is needed because the intra-queue examination only focuses on cross-flow *relative occupancy*. Thus, it cannot identify when flows in the current

Fig. 9 Confucius's
hysteresis reclassification
mechanism for flows. Only
when the buffer occupancy
of a flow has significantly
deviated from the current
class will it be moved to
another class

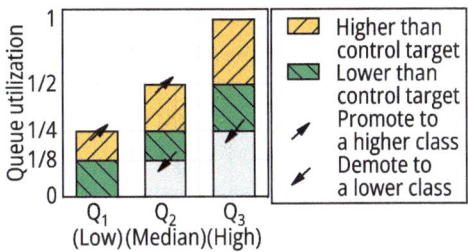

queue are comparably aggressive but more aggressive than the target of this queue.
For example, assume that two Cubic flows were previously classified to Q_1 (the least
aggressive) due to being throttled elsewhere. When these Cubic flows start to be
aggressive, Confucius needs to move them to a different queue to protect incoming
latency-sensitive flows.

6.2 Design Considerations

In practice, Confucius has two following considerations.

Number of queues to set. We observe that the CCAs are concentrated in three clusters
(circles in Fig. 8). Concretely, GCC, Copa, and Vegas have a queue occupancy of less
than 20%; Cubic, Illinois, and Yeah have a queue occupancy of more than 80%; and
BBR stays in-between. Therefore, we set three queues and use the average queue
occupancy in these three clusters as our targets $\{q_0^{(i)}\}$. We expect other CCAs to fall
into one of these three representative categories, if not we can configure Confucius
to work with more queues.

Variation of buffer aggressiveness. A flow's buffer aggressiveness can change over
time. For example, a Cubic flow throttled/congested elsewhere (on a different router)
will not be aggressive in buffer occupancy (although Cubic, the algorithm, would).
Such a Cubic flow can share the queue with other delay-sensitive flows. However,
when the bottleneck moves to the current router, this Cubic flow will be aggressive
on the buffer occupancy, where the flow can no longer share the queue.

7 Confucius Implementation

Implementing Confucius in the Linux kernel has some challenges. We discuss them
and our solutions below.

Order-preserving during reclassification. Flows can be moved to another class
during runtime. Thus, we need to ensure the order-preservation during the reclassification of Confucius of a certain flow. In response, we adopt a virtual class design

in Confucius. During the enqueue process of new packets, we bind the `sk_buff` to each flow. During the dequeue process, we search for all flows that are bound to the determined class and dequeue the packet with the earliest enqueue time. In this way, when moving a flow to another class, we can just rebind the pointer of the flow from the previous class to the new class.

Reducing computational overhead. To implement Confucius in the Linux kernel and optimize the execution overhead, we need to optimize the computational overhead strictly. Specifically, we have the following two implementations:

(i) Bit-shifts for exponential operations. Confucius reweights flows based on their ages with an exponential function, yet the floating number calculation in the kernel is expensive. Therefore, we quantize the weight of new flows with the unit of $\frac{1}{128}$ and use bit shifts for the exponential weight updates, i.e., left shifting the weight by one bit every $\frac{1}{\lambda}$ milliseconds.

(ii) Periodical reweighting and reclassification. The reweighting and reclassification are not necessary for each packet. For the reweighting, we only need to reweight for a flow every $\frac{1}{\lambda}$ milliseconds. When we set $\lambda = 0.004$, this means to reweight every 250 ms. For the reclassification, we should observe the results after moving one flow to a new class for at least one RTT to measure the queue utilization and observe the behavior of the flow in the new class. Therefore, we also reclassify the flows in a periodic way—we set the reclassification interval to 100 ms.

8 Summary

In this chapter, we propose Confucius, the first queue management scheme to balance fairness against volatility. Confucius achieves this by grouping flows based on their latency preferences, which it infers by observing their buffer occupancy over time. Confucius gradually adjusts per-flow weight and uses those weights to devise the per-queue service rate. Doing so allows Confucius to mitigate volatility that degrades the performance of interactive multimedia streaming flows.

References

1. Nichols, K., Jacobson, V.: Controlling queue delay. Communications of the ACM (2012)
2. Lin, D., Morris, R.: Dynamics of random early detection. In Proc, ACM SIGCOMM (1997)
3. Feng, W.C., Kandlur, D., Saha, D., Shin, K.: A new class of active queue management algorithms, Blue (1999)
4. Feng, W. C., Kapadia, A., Thulasidasan, S.: Green: proactive queue management over a best-effort network. In: Proc, IEEE GLOBECOM (2002)
5. Long, C., Zhao, B., Guan, X., Yang, J.: The yellow active queue management algorithm. Elsevier Computer Networks (2005)

6. Spang, B., Arslan, S., McKeown, N.: Updating the theory of buffer sizing. Perform. Eval. **151**, 102232 (2021)

7. Tang, J., Liu, S., Xu, Y., Guo, Z., Zhang, J., Gao, P., Chen, Y., Wang, X., Chao, H.J.: Abs: Adaptive buffer sizing via augmented programmability with machine learning. In: Proc. IEEE INFOCOM, pp. 2038–2047 (2022)

8. Katabi, D., Handley, M., Rohrs, C.: Congestion control for high bandwidth-delay product networks. In: Proc, ACM SIGCOMM (2002)

9. Tai, C. H., Zhu, J., Dukkipati, N.: Making large scale deployment of rcp practical for real networks. In: Proc. IEEE INFOCOM (2008)

10. Flores, M., Wenzel, A., Kuzmanovic, A.: Enabling router-assisted congestion control on the internet. In: Proc, IEEE ICNP (2016)

11. Goyal, P., Agarwal, A., Netravali, R., Alizadeh, M., Balakrishnan, H.: Abc: a simple explicit congestion controller for wireless networks. In: Proc, USENIX NSDI (2020)

12. Floyd, S., Jacobson, V.: Random early detection gateways for congestion avoidance. IEEE/ACM Trans. Netw. (1993)

13. Feng, W.C., Kandlur, D.D., Saha, D., Shin, K.G.: A queue management algorithm for enforcing fairness. In: Proc. IEEE INFOCOM, Stochastic fair blue (2001)

14. Chatranon, G., Labrador, M.A., Banerjee, S.: Black: detection and preferential dropping of high bandwidth unresponsive flows. In: Proc. IEEE ICC (2003)

15. Pan, R., Breslau, L., Prabhakar, B., Shenker, S.: Approximate fairness through differential dropping. ACM SIGCOMM Computer Communication Review **33**(2), 23–39 (2003)

16. Schepper, K.D., Briscoe, B., White, G.: Dual-queue coupled active queue management (AQM) for low latency, low loss, and scalable throughput (L4S). RFC 9332 (2023)

17. Bai, W., Chen, L., Chen, K., Han, D., Tian, C., Wang, H.: Information-agnostic flow scheduling for commodity data centers. In: Proc, USENIX NSDI (2015)

18. Alizadeh, M., Yang, S., Sharif, M., Katti, S., McKeown, N., Prabhakar, B., Shenker, S.: pfabric: minimal near-optimal datacenter transport. In Proc, ACM SIGCOMM (2013)

19. Addanki, V., Apostolaki, M., Ghobadi, M., Schmid, S., Vanbever, L.: Abm: active buffer management in datacenters. In: Proc, ACM SIGCOMM (2022)

20. Baker, F., Babiarz, J., Chan, K.H.: Configuration guidelines for diffserv service classes. IETF RFC 4594 (2006)

21. Tcp analysis | cs-224-lectures. https://grubdragon.github.io/CS-224-Lectures/lec/lec11.html

22. Appenzeller, G., Keslassy, I., McKeown, N.: Sizing router buffers. ACM SIGCOMM Computer Communication Review **34**(4), 281–292 (2004)

23. Carlucci, G., De Cicco, L., Holmer, S., Mascolo, S.: Congestion control for web real-time communication. IEEE/ACM Trans. Netw. (2017)

24. Ray, D., Smith, C., Wei, T., Chu, D., Seshan, S.: Sqp: congestion control for low-latency interactive video streaming. arXiv preprint arXiv:2207.11857 (2022)

25. Arun, V., Balakrishnan, H.: Copa: practical delay-based congestion control for the internet. In: Proc, USENIX NSDI (2018)

26. Rudow, M., Yan, Francis Y., Kumar, A., Ananthanarayanan, G., Ellis, M., Rashmi, K.V.: Stream-melt: efficient loss recovery for videoconferencing via streaming codes. In Proc. USENIX NSDI (2023)

27. Meng, Z., Kong, X., Chen, J., Wang, B., Xu, M., Han, R., Liu, H., Arun, V., Hu, H., Wei, X.: Hairpin: Rethinking packet loss recovery in edge-based interactive video streaming. In: Proc, USENIX NSDI (2024)

28. Wang, H., Yu, Z., Zhang, R., Tao, S., Yu, H., Shi, S.: Twinstar: A practical multi-path transmission framework for ultra-low latency video delivery. In: Proc. ACM Multimedia, pp. 9234-9242 (2023)

29. Ni, Y., Zheng, Z., Lin, X., Gao, F., Zeng, X., Liu, Y., Xu, T., Wang, H., Zhang, Z., Du, S., et al.: Cellfusion: Multipath vehicle-to-cloud video streaming with network coding in the wild. In: Proc. ACM SIGCOMM, pp. 668–683 (2023)

30. Dhawaskar Sathyanarayana, S., Lee, K., Grunwald, D., Ha, S.: Converge: qoe-driven multipath video conferencing over webrtc. In: Proc. ACM SIGCOMM, pp. 637–653 (2023)

31. Meng, Z., Wang, T., Shen, Y., Wang, B., Xu, M., Han, R., Liu, H., Arun, V., Hu, H., Wei, X.: Enabling high quality real-time communications with adaptive frame-rate. In: Proc, USENIX NSDI (2023)
32. Fouladi, S., Emmons, J., Orbay, E., Wu, C., Wahby, R.S., Winstein, K.: Salsify: Low-latency network video through tighter integration between a video codec and a transport protocol. In: Proc. USENIX NSDI (2018)
33. Meng, Z., Guo, Y., Sun, C., Wang, B., Sherry, J., Liu, H. H., Xu, M.: Achieving consistent low latency for wireless real time communications with the shortest control loop. In: Proc. ACM SIGCOMM (2022)
34. Chen, W., Ma, L., Shen, C.C.: Congestion-aware mac layer adaptation to improve video tele-conferencing over wi-fi. In: Proc, ACM MMSys (2015)
35. Chang, H., Varvello, M., Hao, F., Mukherjee, S.: Can you see me now? a measurement study of zoom, webex, and meet. In: Proc. ACM IMC, pp. 216–228 (2021)
36. Michel, O., Sengupta, S., Kim, H., Netravali, R., Rexford, J.: Enabling passive measurement of zoom performance in production networks. In: Proceedings of the 22nd ACM internet measurement conference, pp. 244–260 (2022)
37. Briscoe, B., De Schepper, K., Bagnulo, M., White, G.: Low latency, low loss, and scalable throughput (L4S) internet service: architecture. RFC 9330 (2023)
38. Xiong, Z., Zilberman, N.: Do switches dream of machine learning? toward in-network classi-fication. In: Proc. ACM HotNEts, pp. 25–33 (2019)
39. Li, T., Zheng, K., Xu, K., Jadhav, R. A., Xiong, T., Winstein, K., Tan, K.: Improving wireless transport performance by taming acknowledgments. In: Proc. ACM SIGCOMM, Tack (2020)
40. Xu, X., Claypool, M.: Measurement of cloud-based game streaming system response to com-peting tcp cubic or tcp bbr flows. In: Proc. ACM IMC, pp. 305–316 (2022)
41. Slivar, I., Suznjevic, M., Skorin-Kapov, L.: The impact of video encoding parameters and game type on qoe for cloud gaming: A case study using the steam platform. In: Proc. IEEE international conference on quality of multimedia experience (QoMEX) (2015)
42. Bajpai, V., Eravuchira, S.J., Schönwälder, J.: Dissecting last-mile latency characteristics. ACM SIGCOMM Computer Communication Review **47**(5), 25–34 (2017)
43. Fontugne, R., Shah, A., Cho, K.: Persistent last-mile congestion: not so uncommon. In: Proc. ACM IMC, pp. 420–427 (2020)
44. Tahir, A., Mittal, R.: Enabling users to control their internet. In: Proc. USENIX NSDI, pp. 555–573 (2023)
45. Xu, D., Zhou, A., Zhang, X., Wang, G., Liu, X., An, C., Shi, Y., Liu, L., Ma, H.: Under-standing operational 5g: a first measurement study on its coverage, performance and energy consumption. In: Proc, ACM SIGCOMM (2020)
46. Bhartia, A., Chen, B., Wang, F., Pallas, D., Musaloiu-E, R., Lai, T.T.T., Ma, H.: Measurement-based, practical techniques to improve 802.11 ac performance. In: Proc. ACM IMC (2017)
47. Anurag. What os does the router use? is it linux? - quora https://www.quora.com/What-OS-does-the-router-use-Is-it-Linux#:Ëœ:text=Yes%20most%20of%20the%20router,the %20router%20as%20pre%2Dinstalled.
48. Weidenbach, P., vom Dorp, J.: Home router security report 2020. https://www.fkie.fraunhofer. de/content/dam/fkie/de/documents/HomeRouter/HomeRouterSecurity_2020_Bericht.pdf (2020)
49. Marder, A., Luckie, M., Huffaker, B.,Claffy, K. C.: Inferring persistent interdomain congestion. In: Proc. ACM SIGCOMM pp. 1–15 (2018)
50. ITU Recommendations. G.1070 : Opinion model for video-telephony applications. https:// www.itu.int/rec/T-REC-G.1070 (2018)
51. Netlog: Chrome's network logging system. https://www.chromium.org/developers/design-documents/network-stack/netlog/
52. Meng, Z., Atre, N., Xu, M., Sherry, J., Apostolaki, M.: Confucius queue management: be fair but not too fast. arXiv preprint 2310.18030 (2023)
53. Chen, L., Chen, K., Bai, W., Alizadeh, M.: Scheduling mix-flows in commodity datacenters with karuna. In: Proc, ACM SIGCOMM (2016)

54. Zhou, Y., Wang, T., Wang, L., Wen, N., Han, R., Wang, J., Chenglei, W., Chen, J., Jiang, L., Wang, S., et al.: Augur: Practical mobile multipath transport service for low tail latency in real-time streaming. In: Proc, USENIX NSDI (2024)

55. Xie, Y., Yi, F., Jamieson, K.: Pbe-cc: Congestion control via endpoint-centric, physical-layer bandwidth measurements. In: Proc, ACM SIGCOMM (2020)

56. Lucas, J.M., Saccucci, M.S.: Exponentially weighted moving average control schemes: properties and enhancements. Technometrics $32(1)$, 1–12 (1990)

57. MacGregor, M.H., Shi, W.: Deficits for bursty latency-critical flows: DRR++. In: Proc. IEEE International Conference on Networks (ICON) pp. 287–293

58. Mishra, A., Sun, X., Jain, A., Pande, S., Joshi, R., Leong, B.: The great internet tcp congestion control census. In: Proc, ACM Sigmetrics (2020)

59. Zhang, J., Dong, E., Meng, Z., Yang, Y., Xu, M., Yang, S., Zhang, M., Yue, Y.: Wisetrans: Adaptive transport protocol selection for mobile web service. In: Proceedings of the Web Conference, (2021)

Conclusions and Future Work

Interactive multimedia streaming is a long-standing research topic in network systems, but the application scenarios it faces are becoming more and more complex. From network telephony to video conferencing, to cloud gaming, remote surgery, and finally to virtual reality and augmented reality, the latency requirements of applications for networks are getting higher and higher, and the scenarios are becoming more diverse. Interactive multimedia streaming applications involve a series of deep systemic issues, some of which are not just research problems in the field of networks. This book only addresses some key problems, but there are some aspects that can be further explored in the future.

1. Joint optimization with the operating system. With the gradual deployment of edge node deployment and the large-scale deployment of new-generation wireless access network technologies (such as WiFi 6 and 5G), the net propagation delay of networks is getting lower and lower. At this point, the latency bottleneck on the endpoint side becomes more prominent. Of course, many excellent researchers in the field of operating systems are also trying to reduce this latency, but it should be noted that network latency is actually the most elastic part of latency components: the network can always sacrifice some throughput for lower latency. Therefore, if the latency budget of the entire link can be planned in advance when the endpoint operating system and other latency bottlenecks are anticipated, latency can be further reduced.

2. Joint optimization with different scenarios. Network layer indicators are currently more related to network service quality. Even if the stutter rate and other indicators are actually counted at the application layer video frame granularity, this is not the user's real experience, but only an estimate of the user experience. Furthermore, different users may have different experiences with the same latency and picture quality due to differences in their physiological and psychological states and application usage. How to understand the user's real experience and optimize it, especially when these emerging application scenarios are gradually entering people's field of vision, is also a direction worth further in-depth research.

Z. Meng and M. Xu, *Latency Optimization in Interactive Multimedia Streaming*,
SpringerBriefs in Computer Science, https://doi.org/10.1007/978-981-97-6729-8

From a broader perspective, the latency problem solved in this paper is not only applicable to interactive multimedia streaming. In fact, the design of the transport layer, network layer, and control path in this work can be migrated to other applications with similar low-latency requirements. In recent years, new network scenarios, such as the Internet of Things and connected vehicles, have brought great opportunities to network research. Whether the low-latency optimization in this work can be applied to other network scenarios and whether there are new challenges to be solved are also directions worth exploring in the future.